"Osborne takes up the word *blessing*, wh
in shallow ways, and sets it in its biblical
we are treated to a broad understanding
richness and fullness of the term in its t
fresh and accessible contribution to bib

Thomas R. Schreiner, James Buchanan Harrison Professor of New
Testament Interpretation, The Southern Baptist Theological Seminary

"There can be no greater experience than to be blessed by God. Yet Christians
often have little appreciation of what this means in practice. Thankfully, Osborne brings clarity to this subject by providing an excellent overview of the
biblical teaching on blessing. He skillfully and accessibly navigates the topic,
avoiding pitfalls and helpfully highlighting pastoral implications."

T. Desmond Alexander, Senior Lecturer in Biblical Studies and Director
of Postgraduate Studies, Union Theological College, Belfast; author,
The City of God and the Goal of Creation

"What does it mean to be 'blessed'? Does blessing look different in the Old and
New Testaments? Osborne masterfully addresses these questions, yet most of
all summons us to delight in living in the presence of the one from whom all
blessings flow."

Andrew T. Abernethy, Associate Professor of Old Testament,
Wheaton College

"For those looking for a biblical map of blessing, I commend this thoughtful
volume. As an even-handed guide, William Osborne journeys through Genesis
to Revelation, drawing the reader's attention to many high points. Believers
should rejoice over every spiritual blessing they now enjoy in the exalted Christ."

Benjamin Gladd, Associate Professor of New Testament, Reformed
Theological Seminary

"*Divine Blessing and the Fullness of Life in the Presence of God* is an accessible
reminder of how the Bible—not this cultural moment—defines being 'blessed.'
Osborne nicely unpacks this idea and demonstrates its prominence in the unfolding narrative of both Testaments. Readers will come away encouraged and
enlightened, with a better grasp on the good life that God desires for his people."

Michelle Knight, Assistant Professor of Old Testament and Semitic
Languages, Trinity Evangelical Divinity School

"For too many Christians, 'being blessed' translates to personal gain and prosperity. In *Divine Blessing and the Fullness of Life in the Presence of God*, William Osborne gently disabuses readers of such shallow thinking by making the biblical theology of blessing clear and comprehensible. Even more valuable, he explains why we are prone to process blessing so poorly: we define the concept in terms of what *we* want, not in terms of the everlasting inheritance *God* wants for us. Being blessed is about having our minds and lives transformed by the realization that the eye truly has not seen, nor the ear heard, what God has prepared for those who love him."

Michael S. Heiser, Executive Director and Professor, The Awakening School of Theology and Ministry; Host, *The Naked Bible Podcast*; author, *The Unseen Realm*

"From Genesis to Revelation, William Osborne faithfully traces a biblical theology of blessing. Well-researched and scholarly, the study is accessible to anyone wanting to carefully read and learn about God's plan to bless his people. This is a must-read for a great understanding of the already-not-yet nature of God's present and promised future blessing for his people."

Scott R. Andrews, Senior Pastor, Alliance Bible Fellowship, Boone, North Carolina

"*Blessing* is a concept that Christians bandy about, but what actually is it and how does it work? Osborne does the detective work and demystifies it for us. He takes us on a journey through the Scriptures, noting the major evidence and picking up the more subtle clues. Unsurprisingly, blessing has God's fingerprints all over it. Perhaps surprisingly, though, it is more pervasive than we might imagine."

George Athas, Director of Research, Moore College

"We live in an age when the church is being threatened by the destructive teachings of the prosperity gospel, which emphasizes health, wealth, and might in the present. We can be tempted to swing the pendulum to the other extreme by completely rejecting any material blessing as divine. There are some who even bemoan the biblical term *blessing* because they now associate it with the prosperity gospel. Osborne guards us from this extreme by serving us a rich biblical-theological meal. He traces the theme of blessing throughout Scripture and he rightly argues that God's blessings are relational, spiritual, material, present, and future. Enlarge your understanding of the infinitely vast blessings God has lavished on his people by reading this short treasure."

Dieudonné Tamfu, Executive Director of Cameroon Extension Site and Assistant Professor of Bible and Theology, Bethlehem College & Seminary; author, *2 Peter and Jude* (Africa Bible Commentary Series)

Divine Blessing and the Fullness of
Life in the Presence of God

Short Studies in Biblical Theology

Edited by Dane C. Ortlund and Miles V. Van Pelt

The City of God and the Goal of Creation, T. Desmond Alexander (2018)

Covenant and God's Purpose for the World, Thomas R. Schreiner (2017)

Divine Blessing and the Fullness of Life in the Presence of God, William R. Osborne (2020)

From Chaos to Cosmos: Creation to New Creation, Sidney Greidanus (2018)

The Kingdom of God and the Glory of the Cross, Patrick Schreiner (2018)

The Lord's Supper as the Sign and Meal of the New Covenant, Guy Prentiss Waters (2019)

Marriage and the Mystery of the Gospel, Ray Ortlund (2016)

Redemptive Reversals and the Ironic Overturning of Human Wisdom, G. K. Beale (2019)

The Serpent and the Serpent Slayer, Andrew David Naselli (2020)

The Son of God and the New Creation, Graeme Goldsworthy (2015)

Work and Our Labor in the Lord, James M. Hamilton Jr. (2017)

Divine Blessing and the Fullness of Life in the Presence of God

William R. Osborne

:: CROSSWAY®

WHEATON, ILLINOIS

Divine Blessing and the Fullness of Life in the Presence of God

Copyright © 2020 by William R. Osborne

Published by Crossway
        1300 Crescent Street
        Wheaton, Illinois 60187

Cover design: Jordan Singer

First printing 2020

Printed in the United States of America

Trade paperback ISBN: 978-1-4335-6621-9
ePub ISBN: 978-1-4335-6624-0
PDF ISBN: 978-1-4335-6622-6
Mobipocket ISBN: 978-1-4335-6623-3

Library of Congress Cataloging-in-Publication Data

Names: Osborne, William R., author.
Title: Divine blessing and the fullness of life in the presence of God / William R. Osborne.
Description: Wheaton, Illinois : Crossway, 2020. | Series: Short studies in biblical theology | Includes bibliographical references and index.
Identifiers: LCCN 2020013765 (print) | LCCN 2020013766 (ebook) | ISBN 9781433566219 (trade paperback) | ISBN 9781433566226 (pdf) | ISBN 9781433566233 (mobi) | ISBN 9781433566240 (epub)
Subjects: LCSH: Wealth—Religious aspects—Christianity. | Benediction. | Blessing and cursing.
Classification: LCC BR115.W4 O83 2020 (print) | LCC BR115.W4 (ebook) | DC 234/.13—dc23
LC record available at https://lccn.loc.gov/2020013765
LC ebook record available at https://lccn.loc.gov/2020013766

Crossway is a publishing ministry of Good News Publishers.

BP		29	28	27	26	25	24	23	22	21	20
15	14	13	12	11	10	9	8	7	6	5	4	3	2	1

To Sophia, Eleanor, Moses, and Henry

Contents

Series Preface

Most of us tend to approach the Bible early on in our Christian lives as a vast, cavernous, and largely impenetrable book. We read the text piecemeal, finding golden nuggets of inspiration here and there, but remain unable to plug any given text meaningfully into the overarching storyline. Yet one of the great advances in evangelical biblical scholarship over the past few generations has been the recovery of biblical theology—that is, a renewed appreciation for the Bible as a theologically unified, historically rooted, progressively unfolding, and ultimately Christ-centered narrative of God's covenantal work in our world to redeem sinful humanity.

This renaissance of biblical theology is a blessing, yet little of it has been made available to the general Christian population. The purpose of Short Studies in Biblical Theology is to connect the resurgence of biblical theology at the academic level with everyday believers. Each volume is written by a capable scholar or churchman who is consciously writing in a way that requires no prerequisite theological training of the reader. Instead, any thoughtful Christian disciple can track with and benefit from these books.

Each volume in this series takes a whole-Bible theme and traces it through Scripture. In this way readers not only learn about a given theme but also are given a model for how to read the Bible as a coherent whole.

We have launched this series because we love the Bible, we love the church, and we long for the renewal of biblical theology in the academy to enliven the hearts and minds of Christ's disciples all around the world. As editors, we have found few discoveries more thrilling in life than that of seeing the whole Bible as a unified story of God's gracious acts of redemption, and indeed of seeing the whole Bible as ultimately about Jesus, as he himself testified (Luke 24:27; John 5:39).

The ultimate goal of Short Studies in Biblical Theology is to magnify the Savior and to build up his church—magnifying the Savior through showing how the whole Bible points to him and his gracious rescue of helpless sinners; and building up the church by strengthening believers in their grasp of these life-giving truths.

Dane C. Ortlund and Miles V. Van Pelt

Acknowledgments

I am extremely grateful for the many people who worked to make the publication of this book possible. First, I would like to express my gratitude to my many teachers, both in person and in print, who have shaped my reading of the Scriptures and helped me to grow in recognizing the theological storyline of the Bible. I would also like to thank Drs. Miles Van Pelt and Dane Ortlund for their editorial support of this project; their careful reading no doubt improved this book. Others also read over the volume, and I am especially thankful for my friends and colleagues Jay Todd and Russell Meek, who provided several helpful comments.

I truly appreciate Dr. Eric Bolger, Dean of the College, at College of the Ozarks for his support of this project and many others during my time at the college. The sabbatical provided by College of the Ozarks offered time and energy to devote to finishing this project. I am also grateful for Tyndale Theological Seminary providing me with office space and library access, and for their joyful support of my writing efforts while serving there as a visiting professor.

None of my ideas or projects would ever see completion were it not for the enduring support, patience, and encouragement of my dear wife, Sara. I am also grateful for our four children, who continually prove Psalm 127:3–5 to be true; they indeed are a reward!

Finally, I am eternally thankful to the Lord for his unfailing kindness and tender mercies that have followed me throughout my life. What a joy it has been to reflect on the blessings of God offered to us in the gospel! May he use this book to motivate us to respond with the psalmist: "Blessed be his glorious name forever; / may the whole earth be filled with his glory! / Amen and Amen!" (Ps. 72:19).

Soli Deo Gloria

Introduction

Everyday Blessings

The concept of blessing pervades everyday life in our culture. In 2014, Jessica Bennett provided a comical commentary on social media's obsession with the notion of "being blessed." She quips, "There's nothing quite like invoking holiness as a way to brag about your life. But calling something 'blessed' has become the go-to term for those who want to boast about an accomplishment while pretending to be humble, fish for a compliment, acknowledge a success (without sounding too conceited), or purposely elicit envy. Blessed, 'divine or supremely favored,' is now used to explain that coveted Ted talk invite as well as to celebrate your grandmother's 91st birthday."[1] In many sectors of society, the idea of blessing has been co-opted as a spiritual-but-not-religious key term that aligns all too easily with our country's love affair with moralistic therapeutic deism.[2] As Bennett says, for many people, the term has become simply a way of letting the world know our good fortune while alluding to some far-off divine force at work.

---

1. Jessica Bennett, "They Feel 'Blessed': Blessed Becomes a Popular Hashtag on Social Media," *The New York Times*, May 2, 2014, https://www.nytimes.com/2014/05/04/fashion/blessed-becomes-popular-word-hashtag-social-media.html.

2. See Christian Smith and Melinda L. Denton, *Soul Searching: The Religious and Spiritual Lives of America's Teenagers* (New York: Oxford University Press, 2009); Michael Horton, *Christless Christianity: The Alternative Gospel of the American Church* (Grand Rapids, MI: Baker, 2012).

While *blessing* has climbed the pop charts of Christian terms used outside the church in recent years, it seems that few within the Christian community pause to wonder whether or not this popular notion of blessing is biblically accurate. Sadly, this lack of reflection has left the church vulnerable to those eager to define the concept in ways that are problematic and unreflective of the Bible's presentation. The purpose of this book is to establish a biblical-theological foundation of blessing by presenting a concise biblical theology that leans into how we view ourselves as living blessed lives as citizens of God's kingdom.

For many people, the word *blessing*—or *blessed*—has become inseparable from the Christian movement often referred to as the prosperity gospel. In her book *Blessed: A History of the American Prosperity Gospel*, Kate Bowler cites a Pew Study indicating "that 43 percent of all Christian respondents agreed that the faithful receive health and wealth."[3] It is difficult to draw doctrinal lines around this movement, which sometimes is referred to with phrases such as "the Word of Faith movement" or "name-it-and-claim-it theology."[4] However, regardless of the label, the impact of prosperity teaching on the American church cannot be denied. This impact has expanded well beyond the borders of the United States; through international telecasts and satellite radio stations, the message that God materially blesses the faithful can be heard around the clock on almost every continent.[5]

Unsurprisingly, the prosperity movement is not without its appeals to the authoritative witness of Scripture. Many of these pros-

---

3. Kate Bowler, *Blessed: A History of the American Prosperity Gospel* (New York: Oxford University Press, 2013), 6.

4. See Christopher J. H. Wright, et al., "A Statement on the Prosperity Gospel," The Lausanne Theology Working Group, https://www.lausanne.org/content/a-statement-on-the-prosperity-gospel/.

5. During the writing of this book, other responses to the concept of blessing and the prosperity gospel have emerged. See Tina Boesch, *Given: The Forgotten Meaning and Practice of Blessing* (Colorado Springs, CO: NavPress, 2019); Costi Hinn, *God, Greed, and the (Prosperity) Gospel: How Truth Overwhelms a Life Built on Lies* (Grand Rapids, MI: Zondervan, 2019); David Jones and Russell Woodbridge, *Health, Wealth, and Happiness: How the Prosperity Gospel Overshadows the Gospel of Christ* (Grand Rapids, MI: Kregel, 2017).

perity messages quote the Bible, and books are lined with verse references for "biblical support." Is this, in fact, the Bible's message regarding what it means to be blessed? Does the Bible teach that faithful Christians will experience divine blessing through health and wealth? In order to answer these questions, we must develop a sound biblical theology of blessing. Instead of grabbing one quick verse and claiming that this verse promises prosperity and health, we want to understand the idea of blessing as it is presented within the whole scope of God's word. Just like themes such as law, sacrifice, and covenant, the theme of blessing must be understood within the full biblical story, if it is to be understood biblically at all.

Any serious reader of the Bible quickly realizes that there appears to be a difference in the way the Old Testament speaks about blessing and the way the New Testament presents the idea. Even if we don't hold to a prosperity-like overemphasis on the physical manifestation of old covenant blessings, we can easily engage in over-spiritual explanations of how old covenant physicality is replaced by new covenant spirituality. How do we navigate this transition from divine blessing looking like more cattle and crops to what Paul calls "every spiritual blessing" in Ephesians 1? While there is certainly a transition that takes place within the Bible's presentation of blessing, a biblical-theological approach recognizes that God's blessings have always been *both spiritual and physical*. In both God's initial plan for creation and the eagerly anticipated new heavens and new earth, we see these two aspects of God's benevolence toward his creatures. Divine blessing in the Bible is always physical and spiritual because it is fixed upon the reality of *the fullness of life in the presence of God.*

The message of this book is that divine blessing in the Bible looks like God's creatures experiencing the fullness of life—both physically and spiritually—in his presence. The way human beings experience God's blessing changes with the redemptive storyline that traverses the major peaks of creation, fall, redemption, and final restoration. However, blessing always flows out of God's benevolent creative design for his creatures and coincides with obedience to his will.

The goal of this book is to provide a biblical theology of blessing by examining those references to blessing in the Old and New Testaments, recognizing not only their literary context but also their setting in God's plan of redemption. Brian Rosner has helpfully defined biblical theology as "theological interpretation of Scripture in and for the church. It proceeds with historical and literary sensitivity and seeks to analyze and synthesize the Bible's teaching about God and his relations to the world on its own terms, maintaining sight of the Bible's overarching narrative and Christocentric focus."[6] This book seeks to arrive at the "theological heart"[7] of the Bible's view of divine blessing and listen to that same message that has pulsed through the ages, giving life to the people of God.

In the pages that follow, we will explore in more depth the nuanced meaning of the words used to talk about blessing in the Old Testament and New Testament and fix our eyes on God's design of blessing integrally woven in the creation story (chap. 1). Chapter 2 takes us to the heart of the Old Testament's theology of blessing by examining God's plan to bless the world through one man—Abraham. Chapter 3 will walk through God's covenant relationship with Israel, highlighting the covenant realities of those blessings. Moving across the Bible to the New Testament, we will discuss the nature of blessing and our access to divine blessings as new covenant Christians (chap. 4) and close our biblical theology in chapter 5 glorying in the future promises of God's eternal blessings for his people. As Christians, we have graciously been given all things (Rom 8:31–32), and in that moment that we enter God's presence, we will understand

---

6. Brian S. Rosner, "Biblical Theology," in *New Dictionary of Biblical Theology*, ed. T. D. Alexander et al. (Downers Grove, IL: IVP Academic, 2000), 10.

7. Elmer A. Martens, "Tackling Old Testament Theology," *Journal of the Evangelical Theological Society* 20 (1977): 123.

like never before that to know God's blessing is not just to have "all things" but also to have the one who made them.

Can One Word Do All That?

All languages are strange—to the outsider at least. I had a Greek professor many years ago who had a stock answer to the perennial moaning of young Greek students complaining, "Why did they do it like that? It's so confusing!" My professor would calmly reply, "Long ago Greek mommies taught little Greek babies to say it like that." At the time, his response produced nothing from me but an eye roll, but I have come to see the truth in his reply. Languages work where they are.

I say this because it seems a bit strange to us to use one word to communicate the ideas of God blessing people, people blessing God, and people blessing people. This is seen in a passage like 2 Chronicles 31:8: "When Hezekiah and the princes came and saw the heaps [that is, tithes the king encouraged the people to bring], they blessed the LORD and his people Israel." We find only one verb in this passage (Heb. *wayebaraku*), and it is clear that this one word is capable of expressing both the idea of blessing God and blessing people without an apparent problem for the author. This fluidity is seen in the broader Semitic culture of the ancient Near East. The Akkadian word for blessing and praise is *karābu* (reversed consonants from *brk*), which also denotes a two-way stream of blessing from god to worshiper and worshiper to god. "The same Hebrew (*brk*) or Akkadian (*karābu*) verb expresses both the divine act of blessing and the human reaction of praise. Blessing and praise are among the forms of theological expression and thought that tie Israel firmly to the Ancient Near East."[8] Other comparable verb roots appear in Ugaritic, Phoenician-Punic, and Aramaic, all linking blessing to various

---

8. Reinhard Feldmeier and Hermann Spieckermann, *God of the Living: A Biblical Theology*, trans. Mark E. Biddle (Waco, TX: Baylor University Press, 2011), 272.

deities in similar fashion.[9] It is quite common for different languages to not have a one-to-one correspondence when it comes to words and concepts. This fluidity can be seen in the following chart that summarizes the basic meanings of the different forms of the Hebrew root *brk* and the Greek word *eulogeō*:

1. To Bless as an Action
barak: 256 times in the Old Testament; *eulogeō*: thirty times in the New Testament; *eneulogeō*: two times in the New Testament; *kateulogeō*: one time in the New Testament[10]

- God blesses creation and humanity
- God blesses people through other people
- People bless God

2. A Blessing as a Thing
berakah: seventy-one times in the Old Testament; *eulogia*: fifteen times in the New Testament

- That which is conferred by the action of blessing: "to bless a blessing"
- A gift that is given

3. Being Blessed as a State of Being
baruk: seventy-one times in the Old Testament; *eulogeō* middle/passive: eleven times in the New Testament; *eulogētos*: eight times in the New Testament

- Formula-like expression ascribed to God: "Blessed be the Lord."

---

9. Keith N. Grüneberg, *Abraham, Blessing and the Nations: A Philological and Exegetical Study of Genesis 12:3 in Its Narrative Context*, Beihefte zur Zeitschrift für die alttestamentliche Wissenschaft 332 (Berlin: De Gruyter, 2003), 94.

10. For statistics, Ernst Jenni and Claus Westermann, *Theological Lexicon of the Old Testament*, trans. Mark E. Biddle (Peabody, MA: Hendrickson, 1997), 1:266.

- Formula-like expression ascribed to people: "Blessed is the person who . . ."
- Formula-like greeting or kind gesture

Identifying these three general patterns associated with the forms of blessing in the Old Testament will prove helpful as we move forward in our discussion of blessing.[11] Focusing on the three uses of blessing as an action (number 1 in the chart), we will see the interconnectedness of these ideas as well as their distinct nuances. To be clear, there are other words that occur in parallel statements with *brk*-words in the Old Testament, such as "favor" (Heb. *ratson*) and "multiply" (Heb. *ravah*), but there is no doubt that *brk* is the most significant word group used to describe blessing in the Bible.[12] Consequently, once we begin to understand the unique functions of blessing in the Old Testament, then we can see how those categories and ideas are carried into the New Testament with the use of Greek words like *eulogeō* and *makarios*, the former being the most common word used to translate *brk* in the Greek translation of the Old Testament.[13]

God Blesses Creation and Humanity

The first actor in Scripture is God. He acts to create, form, divide, and bless (Gen. 1:22, 28; 2:3). In fact, his blessing reveals a continuous aspect of his first creative energies. His blessing ensures that what was formed and fashioned continues in accordance with his design, will, and creative power. "Blessing is the center of life; it is life itself and

---

11. Christopher W. Mitchell, *The Meaning of BRK "To Bless" in the Old Testament*, SBL Dissertation Series 95 (Atlanta: Scholars, 1987), 165–71.

12. In his thorough analysis, Aitken lists several synonyms for cursing, but when he addresses blessing, only deals with the words associated with *brk*. See James K. Aitken, *The Semantics of Blessing and Cursing in Ancient Hebrew*, Ancient Near Eastern Studies Supplement 23 (Louvain: Peeters, 2007).

13. Jonathan T. Pennington, *The Sermon on the Mount and Human Flourishing: A Theological Commentary* (Grand Rapids, MI: Baker, 2017), 47–48.

includes all phases of life," states Claus Westermann.[14] Therefore, in the Bible, God is the fountainhead and source of all blessings. But God's act of blessing does not just entail the giving of things; it necessitates a right relationship between the two parties—God and his creation. To be blessed by God is to be in right standing with him. God's blessing is experienced by his creatures in two primary categories: creation and covenant. It is in both of these divinely established contexts that God's creatures come to know him as the God who blesses.

However, to say that blessing denotes a relationship is not to downplay the reality of the blessing itself. Blessing often communicates the idea of tangible benefits on the part of the recipient, and this is because "the Old Testament does not relegate divine activity to some 'spiritual' realm, discontinuous with the physical world."[15] As stated earlier, God's involvement in blessing humanity has always been both physical and spiritual. His desire to bless encompasses all that we are as creatures—whole beings, body and soul—created for his glory.

God's blessing is expressed in his people experiencing the fullness of life in his presence, a notion that is frequently communicated by the idea of fertility in the Old Testament. For example, as the source of life, God provided generational longevity in the form of children, abundant harvests in new growth and consistent rain, and multiplication of livestock (the basic meaning of number 2 in the chart). This wholeness, or *shalom*, is characteristic of the blessed state. God's people, by being in right relationship with him, come to know the physical realities of *shalom*, which testify to their unique status as those who are blessed (the basic meaning of number 3 in the chart). The following chapters will explore God's activity in blessing his creation and his people.

---

14. Claus Westermann, *Blessing in the Bible and the Life of the Church*, trans. Keith Crim, Overtures to Biblical Theology (Philadelphia: Fortress, 1978), 18.

15. Grüneberg, *Abraham, Blessing and the Nations*, 94.

God Blesses People through Other People

In other places in the Bible, we encounter another portrait of divine blessing, namely God blessing people through other people. In the Old Testament this form of blessing was mainly carried out by priests or prophets. Deuteronomy 21:5 reads, "Then the priests, the sons of Levi, shall come forward, for the LORD your God has chosen them to minister to him and to bless in the name of the LORD." And we certainly cannot overlook the fascinating chain of events in Balak's spoiled attempt at cursing the people of Israel by the mouth of the prophet Balaam in Numbers 22–24. In numerous places in the Old Testament, God chooses to speak words of blessing through the lips of others and to take up human agency as a means for accomplishing his blessings.

Once we begin to think about people blessing other people, some important questions arise that deserve our attention. If someone is verbally blessed by another person, is God obligated to do something? Is there a latent power in the words of the blessing that are being harnessed by a superspiritual person? Does speaking something make it real? Some scholars have argued that this view of blessings and curses is rooted in an ancient worldview of magic and incantations, where spoken words were believed to become an operative force in the world.[16] However, while there is no denying the ancient, magic-filled worldview revealed in numerous ancient sources, there is no reason to assume that the Old Testament operates in the same fashion. While both ancient Israel and its neighbors lived and thought in a world dominated by what we call "supernatural"

---

16. An influential work arguing this view is Johannes Pedersen, *Israel, Its Life and Culture* (London: Oxford, 1926), 99–181. See Mitchell's helpful summary in *The Meaning of BRK "To Bless,"* 17–20. In the ancient world, many cultures believed that certain blessings were a means of protection that warded off evil spirits or forces. Prayers and blessings were often tied to religious rituals and sacrifices designed to care for the gods and ensure the well-being of the supplicant (see Karen Rhea Nemet-Nejat, *Daily Life in Ancient Mesopotamia* [Peabody, MA: Hendrickson, 1998], 189–90).

activity, one primary difference is the source of authority and power of divine blessing. The narrative account of Balaam and Balak reinforces the idea that all human blessings had their source in God, not some human-initiated incantation or self-fulfilled prophecy.[17] The blessing in Israel was a theological phenomenon, but it was also a cultural one, governed by societal norms and ways of life. This is not to diminish the theological power behind the blessing, but it is important to understand that—like covenants—blessings had cultural currency as well.

As with sacrifice (which also existed outside ancient Israel), blessings and sacrifices were Israel's proper response to God's revelation and were always to function in accordance with that revelation. They were not intended to please the emotionally volatile gods or convince them to make their will known or to act, as with other cultures. One of the unique characteristics of Israel's religion in the ancient world was the fact that Israel was called to imitate and coidentify with the person and character of its God.[18] Israel's God was a blessing God, and we should not be surprised that the God who said, "Be holy, for I the Lord your God am holy" (Lev. 19:2), calls his people to bless the world he created.

The contemporary Word of Faith position promoted by many prosperity teachers also holds that there is a latent divine power in words when the faithful speak them out loud—thus the adage "when you confess, you possess." Briefly, there are some significant problems with this view of people speaking blessings. Biblically, God is the source of power of all spoken blessings in the Bible, and words function as the channel or means for God's blessing, not the source

---

17. The person who utters a blessing does not "effect blessing" or bring it about by some inherent force in the words themselves, whether that force be seen as magical, religious, or psychological.

18. John Walton, *Ancient Near Eastern Thought and the Old Testament: Introducing the Conceptual World of the Hebrew Bible*, 2nd ed. (Grand Rapids, MI: Baker, 2018), 71.

of it. Are words powerful? Yes. They can shape the way we perceive ourselves, our surroundings, and our relationships. What we say deeply affects us and those around us—so that we can bless others with our grace-filled words. However, this does not mean that our words deliver a religious ultimatum to God. Many times in Scripture, when the people of God assume divine favor because of their covenant relationship with God, things don't go very well—like that time when the people of Israel believed that because they had the ark and God's presence, they couldn't possibly lose in battle, yet they lost (1 Sam. 4–5). And that time when the residents of Jerusalem believed the city couldn't possibly fall because they had the temple, yet the city fell (Jer. 7:1–10). People in the Bible certainly ask for blessings from others, but one can only bless God or bless others—not bless themselves. Believing that our words, or the words of a leader, create a reality that God has "promised" us without having scriptural support of such promises is simply foolhardy and presumptuous.

In the Old Testament, the significance of a blessing is grounded more in the person speaking the blessing than the content of the blessing uttered. So blessings—like prayers—were given differing weight based upon the person speaking them and the context in which they were said. The words "I do" have much more significance when spoken by couples adorned in white dresses and tuxedos than they might with two college students answering "Do you love me?" over a cup of coffee. A person might utter a word of blessing as an everyday greeting or when sending someone off on a good journey, whereas these same words would have had much more gravitas when uttered by the priest over the people gathered before the temple, or a father at the birth of a child.

The more authority the speakers have, the more weight is given to the blessing. Priests, prophets, and parents (e.g., Hannah and Mary) all have a God-given authority, and pronounce blessings petitioning

God to act with that authority. Not all human blessings in the Old Testament were uttered by priests. In fact, it seems that anyone could utter a blessing as a sendoff or greeting, such as Rebekah's brothers in Genesis 24:60.

The priestly prayer with which Aaron is instructed to bless the people in Numbers 6:22–27 provides a valuable glimpse into God blessing people through people. The passage reads:

> The LORD spoke to Moses, saying, "Speak to Aaron and his sons, saying, Thus you shall bless the people of Israel: you shall say to them,
>
>> The LORD bless you and keep you;
>> the LORD make his face to shine upon you and be
>>   gracious to you;
>> the LORD lift up his countenance upon you and give
>>   you peace.
>
> So shall they put my name upon the people of Israel, and I will bless them."

God's desire is to bless his people, and he initiates that blessing by establishing a priesthood that would *speak* the words of blessing over the people. In this passage Aaron functions as a mediator—or conduit—of God's blessing. The words he is instructed to speak highlight the necessary relational aspect of divine blessing. What does it mean for Aaron to bless the people? In effect, he is calling on God to protect, to show favor, to be gracious, to grant wholeness, and consequently to mark out Israel as God's singular chosen people. And as God's people today, Christians continue to experience this type of mediated blessing in worship services where the leader stands and offers a benediction, proclaiming a blessing or a "good word" over the congregation. Experiencing God's relational favor is knowing his blessing, and the priest was to bless the people, bridging the relational space created by human sinfulness.

People Bless God

It is primarily in the worship literature of the Psalms that the language of blessing gets redirected from people back to God. The word *bless* is used synonymously with praise in several passages.

> I will *bless* the LORD at all times;
> > his *praise* shall continually be in my mouth. (Ps. 34:1)

> *Bless* the LORD, O my soul!
> *Praise* the LORD! (Ps. 104:35)

> Every day I will *bless* you
> > and *praise* your name forever and ever. (Ps. 145:2)

God's people not only actively bless him through their praise; they also declare him as the one who is blessed and should be blessed (the basic meaning of number 3 in the chart). The justification of his blessing is grounded in numerous factors: he hears (Ps. 28:6), shows steadfast love (Ps. 31:21), saves (Ps. 68:19), and does wondrous things (Ps. 72:18). God's great acts of salvation and deliverance prompt his people to respond with blessing, and the psalmists repeatedly call the people (even themselves, see Ps. 103) to praise the one God worthy of all blessing.

Blessing in the New Testament

As stated earlier, the main words used in the New Testament to communicate notions of blessing are *eulogeō* and *makarios*. Greek translators of the Old Testament choose the former, from where we get the

English word *eulogy*, when rendering texts that use the forms of *brk* we have identified. To be clear, there is a noticeable shift from the place of prominence blessing plays in the Old Testament Scriptures and the New Testament. The Greek verb *eulogeō*, "to bless," occurs only forty-one times in the New Testament, and is found primarily in Hebrews, Luke, Matthew, and Mark.[19] The noun "blessing" (*eulogia*) and the adjective "blessed" (*eulogētos*) occur less often: sixteen times for the former and eight times for the latter. While the theme of blessing certainly continues, it does indeed shift in prominence and focus. This fact demonstrates why it is important for us to remember that words don't equal concepts. Divine blessing continues to play a role in God's plan of redemption in the New Testament, but the language and ideas change.

As Jewish history continues to unfold between the times of the Old Testament and New Testament, the use of blessings comes to center more upon the idea of blessing as a statement uttered by one person over another—that is, a benediction. We find a blessing delivered by the instructor to Jews living at Qumran similar to that given by the Old Testament priests:

> May the Lord bless you from His holy habitation; may He throw open for you an everlasting fount from heaven, never failing. . . . May He grace you with every blessing of the heavenlies; may He teach you the knowledge of the angels! . . . May He open for you an eternal fount; may He never withhold living water from the thirsty. You shall be. . . . May He deliver you from all your enemies; may He smite whom you hate so that none survive. (1QSb, I, 3–7)[20]

---

19. Moisés Silva, ed. *New International Dictionary of New Testament Theology and Exegesis*, 2nd ed. (Grand Rapids, MI: Zondervan, 2014), 2:323.

20. Cited from Michael O. Wise, Martin G. Abegg Jr., and Edward M. Cook, *The Dead Sea Scrolls: A New Translation* (New York: HarperOne, 1996), 141. I have deleted brackets from the original translation.

Jews continued to take up the psalms in their corporate worship in the centuries following the Old Testament period, and in doing so, the connection between blessing and praising God becomes more and more solidified.[21] When we get to Jesus blessing in the Gospels, he is declaring a blessing over children or a meal, reflecting the close relationship between blessing and specific prayers. If the theme of blessing in the Old Testament centered upon the divine activity of God blessing humanity, the New Testament focus of blessing points to the significance of who has received blessing (number 2 in the chart) and consequently who is blessed (number 3 in the chart).

Conclusion

Having completed some important groundwork about the three primary uses of the language of *blessing* in the Bible, we are now prepared to move forward in developing a biblical theology of blessing. As we turn our attention to the book of Genesis in the next chapter and begin to reflect on the theme of divine blessing in the Bible, we will begin to move through the storyline of the Bible, following God's plan of redemption from creation to new creation, analyzing the various ways the theme of God's blessing emerges from the text, and developing a Christ-centered theological synthesis that shows Jesus and his kingdom as the highpoint and fulfillment of God's desire to bless the world.

---

21. The early Jewish text *Mishnah Berakhot* (lit. "Blessings") describes the teachings of the rabbis with regard to required prayers and blessings. The two terms are used nearly synonymously. See https://www.sefaria.org /Mishnah_Berakhot.2?lang=bi.

1

Blessing and Curse, Life and Death

When I was growing up, I spent many weeks of the summer riding my bike in a church parking lot, and it didn't take long for boredom to cause me to begin looking for scrap pieces of wood to build a ramp. My early engineering experiments in ramp building taught me rather quickly that trajectory (a term I didn't know at the time, but a concept I became painfully familiar with) was a critical component of determining where and how one lands. With many scrapes and bruises, I started to see that where and how you take off has everything to do with where you end up. The same is true for biblical theology. We must first direct much of our attention to building a proper understanding of God's design for his world if we are going to understand how the biblical story unfolds.

The first three chapters of Genesis are critical territory for any biblical-theological discussion. In fact, they serve as the foundation of what is often called a "biblical worldview." That is, they begin the universal story of the world that answers fundamental questions like: Who are we? Where did we come from? How are we to live? What is wrong with the world? And how can it be fixed?[1] This story unfolds in the opening chapters of Genesis, revealing God's initial design, or the divine blueprint, for all of creation.[2] Graeme Goldsworthy calls this "the pattern of the kingdom"—namely, all of creation existed in perfect relationship with its sovereign king.[3] However, anyone familiar with these first chapters knows that this perfect relationship does not last long. God's good world is quickly marred by human rebellion. Genesis 1–3 sets us on a trajectory of understanding God's original design of giving abundant life to be experienced in his presence, and the tragic consequences of cursing that followed humanity's chafing against that design.

God Creates to Give Life

The Bible begins with God's existence as a foregone conclusion. God's origins are not defined, defended, or discussed. Old Testament theologian Ludwig Köhler was right when he stated, "The assumption that God exists is the Old Testament's greatest gift to mankind."[4] So, we begin with that gift—God exists and is the source of everything else that comes into existence. Interestingly, these are the very ideas associated with God's self-revelation of his name to Moses in Exodus 3:14: "I AM WHO I AM." He is the one who exists and acts on behalf of his people. God's very nature is Trinitarian, relational, eternal, and outward oriented, and because of this, creation came into existence by the word of God as an overflow of his character.[5] Consequently, God's creating is inseparably tied to his blessing, as we see in the first chapters of Genesis.

---

1. C. John Collins, *Reading Genesis Well: Navigating History, Poetry, Science, and Truth in Genesis 1–11* (Grand Rapids, MI: Zondervan, 2018), 135.

2. Elmer Martens, *God's Design: A Focus on Old Testament Theology*, 4th ed. (Eugene, OR: Wipf & Stock, 2015), 19–21.

3. Graeme Goldsworthy, *According to Plan: The Unfolding Revelation of God in the Bible* (Downers Grove, IL: IVP, 1991), 99.

4. Ludwig Köhler, *Old Testament Theology*, trans. A. S. Todd (London: Lutterworth, 1957; repr. Cambridge: James Clarke, 2002), 19.

5. Michael Horton, *The Christian Faith: A Systematic Theology for Pilgrims on the Way* (Grand Rapids, MI: Zondervan, 2011), 329.

CREATION AND BLESSING LIVING CREATURES

Genesis 1 describes God's creative power as he calls forth light and darkness, earth and sky, and even celestial bodies. The world that was once "without form and void" (1:2), is shaped and prepared for the habitation of life, and ultimately human life. The living God is the life-giving God. On day five of the narrative (1:20–21), God creates sea creatures great and small, along with the birds of the air.

It is during the events of day five that we are introduced to the notion of divine blessing for the first time in the Bible. After God witnessed the goodness of what he had made, the text says, "And God blessed them, saying 'Be fruitful and multiply and fill the waters in the seas, and let birds multiply on the earth'" (Gen. 1:22). God's blessing conferred his design and intent over his creatures. In this way, the divine blessing serves as an extension of God's creative activity. The act of pronouncing a blessing in Genesis 1:22 looks like God commanding his creation to "be fruitful," "multiply," and "fill" within the context he created them. James McKeown writes, "In this context [these verbs] are used together to give maximum prominence to the concept that the creator's blessing would lead to a world teeming with life."[6] We will see that these verbs reappear through the book of Genesis (1:28; 8:17; 9:1, 7), providing thematic cohesion to the narrative of God's plan to bless the world.

CREATION AND BLESSING IMAGE-BEARING PEOPLE

As important as this first divine blessing is, day six presents the pinnacle of God's creative, life-giving project. After creating land animals according to their kinds, we are told that God created mankind in his image (Gen. 1:24–26). In verses 1:27 and 28, as in 1:21–22, there is a close connection between God's work of creation and his blessing:

---

6. James McKeown, *Genesis*, The Two Horizons Old Testament Commentary (Grand Rapids, MI: Eerdmans, 2008), 226.

"So God created. . . . And God blessed." While it is true that the creation account is always progressing toward its Sabbath-resolution, according to the narrative structure, the creation of humanity stands at the highest peak of the story's terrain.[7] The creation of human life stands out against the origin of fish and animal life because God created humanity *in his image, and he blessed them*. What does this often used yet enigmatic phrase, "in his image," mean? (1) Humanity was to have a certain kind of life, one that reflected its Maker by exercising dominion and authority as his vice-regents. (2) His image bearers were to reflect their Maker's reign in the world over all other living things, thereby giving glory to their Creator. (3) As those coreigning with their Maker, humanity was to have a unique relationship with God. From the moment of creation, what it means to be human can only ever be understood in proper relationship to God. And (4) humanity shares spiritual characteristics with God.[8] Genesis 2:7 speaks of God taking the man from the ground and breathing the "breath of life" into his nostrils. This is a profound picture of God's life-giving breath to the first human being.

As he did with the sea creatures on the fifth day, God also declares a blessing over humanity in Genesis 1:28, which is often referred to as the *cultural mandate*. After the climatic declaration that humanity will bear his image (1:27), the text says, "And God blessed them. And God said to them, 'Be fruitful and multiply and fill the earth and subdue it, and have dominion over the fish of the sea and over the birds of the heavens and over every living thing that moves on the earth.'" As we saw in 1:22, God's blessing is a spoken word

---

7. Gordon J. Wenham, *Genesis 1–15*, Word Biblical Commentary 1 (Nashville, TN: Thomas Nelson, 1987), 38; Allen P. Ross, *Creation & Blessing: A Guide to the Study and Exposition of Genesis* (Grand Rapids, MI: Baker, 1998), 113; Collins, *Reading Genesis Well*, 163; Kenneth A. Mathews, *Genesis 1–11:26*, New American Commentary 1A (Nashville, TN: Broadman & Holman, 1996), 160.

8. Robin Routledge, *Old Testament Theology: A Thematic Approach* (Nottingham: Apollos, 2013), 140–41.

given *to* his people. McKeown notes that the words "to them" are included in verse 28 but excluded in the blessing of the sea creatures and birds, indicating in that while "God blesses other creatures, it is the blessing on the humans that reflects the more intimate relations."[9]

The blessing of Genesis 1:28 also encompasses multiplication and fertility just like the blessing spoken over the sea creatures and birds. While this notion of blessing may feel culturally distant from us in the twenty-first century, fertility and procreation are central features of divine blessing, especially in Genesis.[10] The fulfillment of God's blessing in 1:28 requires the one-flesh union of the man and the woman that we read about in 2:21–25.[11] However, as we will see, the themes of fruitfulness and multiplication extend beyond Genesis and provide a narrative cohesion to the story of Israel.[12] God's blessing of humanity is directly tied to mankind's function as his image bearers. The divine plan is that God's image bearers fill the earth, exercising authority and dominion over the earth, with the result that the earth is filled with the image and glory of its Creator.

God's spoken benediction over his creatures is both liberating and binding. The text states that God blessed them, but the blessing includes a series of commands: be fruitful, multiply, fill, subdue, and have dominion. He blesses them to live the life he gave them to the fullest, but he simultaneously establishes divine definitions as to what that "blessed" life can look like. For the biblical author and audience, there is no tension found in the idea that God's blessing would include divine directives. While these first words

---

9. McKeown, *Genesis*, 222.

10. Claus Westermann, *Blessing in the Bible and the Life of the Church*, trans. Keith Crim (Philadelphia: Fortress, 1978), 18.

11. "It is precisely because fertility and marriage are considered as natural gifts bestowed on the creature (nature not being understood in any ideological sense of self-sufficiency), that the Old Testament reacts very sharply against any unnatural perversion of these God-given gifts" (Walther Zimmerli, *The Old Testament and the World*, trans. J. J. Scullion [London: SPCK, 1976], 35).

12. Collins, *Reading Genesis Well*, 112.

of blessing may not appear to occur within an explicit covenantal setting, throughout Israel's history God's revealed command was always perceived as a blessing to his people (see Ps. 119:1–25). The divine directives of Genesis 1:22 and 28 are not covenant stipulations like those presented later in Israel's covenantal interactions with the Lord, but they are creation commands that reveal God's intentions for his good creation. The "blessed" life is that fullness of life which corresponds to God's good design.

In Genesis 2, we learn that mankind is not only made in God's image, but also made from the earth. The striking scene of God fashioning the man from the ground demonstrates the fundamental material nature of humanity. God has breathed his breath into humans, but we are simultaneously people of the earth. As creatures, we are a complex unity—both spiritual and physical beings—and a proper understanding of God's blessing toward humanity must take this into account.[13] "The Bible makes man a unity: acting, thinking and feeling with his whole being. This living creature, then, and not some distillation from him, is an expression or transcription of the eternal, incorporeal creator in terms of temporal, bodily, creaturely existence."[14] It is not a digression to discuss the nature of humanity in a book about divine blessing. As we have seen, God's blessing of his creatures is inseparable from what he made them to be.

CREATION AND BLESSING THE SEVENTH DAY

Genesis 2:1–3 describes a different kind of blessing than what we encountered in 1:22 and 28, or at least a different type of object being blessed. Having created the world in six days, God observes that the whole project is indeed very good, and then he ceases from his cre-

---

13. Westermann, *Blessing in the Bible*, 19.
14. Derek Kidner, *Genesis*, Tyndale Old Testament Commentary (Downers Grove, IL: IVP, 1967), 55.

ative work on the seventh day.[15] Genesis 2:3 reads, "So God blessed the seventh day and made it holy, because on it God rested from all his work that he had done in creation." What immediately stands out against earlier blessings is that this passage presents the blessing through a narrator telling us that "God blessed" without any notion of a spoken benediction. And second, the recipient of the blessing is not a living creature, but a day. What does it mean to bless a day? At first glance it may seem counterintuitive that God would "bless" the day on which he stopped his creative work, especially given the close connection between the terms "create" and "bless" on days five and six.

However, the blessing is not set against God's creative work; it is the celebration and consecration of his work! First, we must recognize several features that set the seventh day apart from other days in the creation account: (1) there is no introductory "And God;" (2) the parallel structure of days one through three and four through six leaves out the last day; (3) there is no "and there was evening and there was morning" formula; and (4) there is a clear emphasis on the ceasing of creative work over against it being carried out.[16] The day is set apart from a literary perspective, as well as by divine decree.

Second, there is a two-verb pattern in the blessing statements in 1:22, 28, and 2:3:

And God blessed . . . saying (1:22)
And God blessed. . . . And God said (1:28)
And God blessed. . . . And God made it holy (2:3)

In chapter 1 God blessed by proclaiming a blessing, and in chapter 2 he blessed by making the seventh day holy. The holiness of the day is what drives the Mosaic understanding of the passage in Exodus

---

15. There is much confusion over the notion of "rest" in Gen. 2:1–3, especially when people wonder why the all-powerful God of the universe needed a break! The Hebrew word often translated as "rest" primarily communicates the idea that God stopped or ceased from his work.

16. Mathews, *Genesis 1–11:26*, 176.

20:8–11 when Israel is commanded to "remember the Sabbath day, to keep it holy." Mathews rightly connects these two passages.

> The seventh day of creation as a consequence is viewed as God's "sabbath"; thus for the Hebrews Sabbath takes on cosmic meaning. By the commemoration of "Sabbath," God and his creatures share in the celebration of the good creation, and God's people are enjoined to enter into the rhythm of work and joyful rest. Embracing God's sabbath rest meant experiencing the sense of completeness and well being God had accomplished at creation in behalf of all human life.[17]

The blessing and consecration of the seventh day are reflected in the divine pattern for creation, and later concretized in Israel's legal portrayal of God's divine expectations for his people. The law given at Mount Sinai would later make explicit for Israel what God had declared at creation.

God Creates to Dwell

A PLACE FOR PROVISION

The narrative begun in Genesis 2:4 carries the creation account of Genesis 1 forward,[18] focusing our attention on the creation of the man and woman and God's good provision for them in a garden. While Genesis 1 presents us with a broader, almost categorical, introduction to the question "What is a human being?" the garden account of Genesis 2 shows a detailed picture of how human beings came to be in his world and how they are to relate to God and other people.

After God created the man, he planted a garden. The two were made for one another! The design of the garden gave food, water, and

---

17. Mathews, *Genesis 1–11:26*, 180.
18. Nahum Sarna, *Genesis*, JPS Torah Commentary (Philadelphia: Jewish Publication Society, 1989), 16.

shade to the man (Gen. 2:9), and the man was placed in the garden to care for it (2:15). God's provision of life for humanity is further illustrated in the placement of the tree of life in the midst of the garden. Based upon Genesis 3:22, it seems as though humanity's access to the tree of life was part of the early picture of eternal life. As long as they could partake of the tree of life, they could live forever—they could thrive eternally.

A PLACE FOR WORSHIP

The garden in Eden was not just for Adam and his wife. Many biblical scholars have noted that the garden reflects a dwelling place for God as well. As John Walton notes, "The presence of God was the key to the garden and was understood by author and audience as a given from the ancient worldview. His presence is seen as the fertile source of all life-giving waters."[19] The garden in Eden is better understood as a temple-garden, in which the Lord would dwell among his people.[20] God's dwelling with his people is a central feature to the creational picture of divine blessing. As Matt Champlin rightly says, "Whatever else it implies (fertility, life, riches, etc.), relationship with God is always the pivot point of blessing."[21]

Old Testament scholar Gordon Wenham argued several years ago that many significant features of the garden were duplicated or reimaged later in Israel's tabernacle and temple. Some of these features include God walking in the garden (Gen. 3:8; cf. Lev. 26:12; Deut. 23:14; 2 Sam. 7:6–7), the presence of a cherub east of the garden and their presence in the tabernacle and temple, with the entrance being from the east (cf. Ex. 26:31; 1 Kings 6:23–28), and the description of

---

19. John H. Walton, "Eden, Garden of," in *Dictionary of the Old Testament: Pentateuch*, ed. T. Desmond Alexander and David W. Baker (Downers Grove, IL: IVP, 2003), 205.

20. T. Desmond Alexander, *From Eden to the New Jerusalem: An Introduction to Biblical Theology* (Grand Rapids, MI: Kregel, 2008), 21.

21. Matt Champlin, "A Biblical Theology of Blessing in Genesis," *Themelios* 42, no. 1 (2017): 67.

the man's work in Genesis 2:15 ("to work it and keep it") employing the same language used to describe the priests' duties in the tabernacle (cf. Num. 3:7–8; 8:26; 18:5–6).[22]

Recognizing the temple-garden nature of the garden in Eden is important. The garden is the location where God's divine blessing is to play out. "God's original blueprint is for the whole earth to become a temple-city filled with people who have a holy or priestly status,"[23] and this blueprint hinges on humanity's access to the presence of God. To be in God's presence is not merely describing a spatial proximity to him (especially since God is spirit), but to be in his presence is to be relationally near him. Adam and Eve can experience the fullness of life only within the relational presence of the God they were created to worship. It is from this temple-garden that God would bestow his blessing upon his creatures.[24] Consequently, the Bible presents Adam and Eve as royal priests in the garden of God, vice-regents exercising dominion, worshiping, and guarding the temple in the context of divine blessing.

God Creates to Bless

A Prominent Theme

As we have seen, God's initial disposition toward the world he created—especially humanity—is one of blessing. The first two chapters of Genesis reveal a universal divine intention to see mankind experience the fullness of life in God's presence in the garden. The three blessings found in the creation narrative in 1:1–2:3 highlight the importance of this theme at the creation of the world and rise to a three-part chorus: God created to bless.[25]

---

22. Gordon J. Wenham, "Sanctuary Symbolism in the Garden of Eden Story," in *Proceedings of the Ninth World Congress of Jewish Studies, Division A: The Period of the Bible* (Jerusalem: World Union of Jewish Studies, 1986), 19–25.

23. Alexander, *From Eden to the New Jerusalem*, 30.

24. Westermann, *Blessing in the Bible*, 35.

25. Champlin, "A Biblical Theology of Blessing in Genesis," 64.

Genesis 1–2 prioritizes God's declaration of blessing, revealing that God's primary intention was not to present a two-fold option of either blessing or cursing, but a singular disposition of benevolence and enduring provision. The cultural mandate of Genesis 1:28 indicates that the command spoken with the blessing will happen. God will see to it. Even when the man and woman rebel against God, they continue to carry out the commands of 1:28 with God's enabling power.

A MISUNDERSTOOD THEME

Having spent some time describing God's good plan to bless his world and create image bearers who would rule as his vice-regents on the earth, let's make sure there is no confusion here with what others have said about these ideas. Popular televangelist Joel Osteen writes, "When God breathed his life into you, He put a crown on your head. . . . This crown represents your authority. It represents God's blessing and favor on your life. . . . When you're wearing your crown, you'll have a sense of entitlement, thinking, *I have a right to be blessed. I have a right to live in victory*."[26]

On the contrary, we must recognize that God's act of blessing humanity in creation does not place him under obligations to his creatures (see Acts 17:24–25), and human beings are not "owed" a certain fullness of life. To say that we have a "right" to be blessed necessarily implies that someone is therefore obligated to observe that right and "bless us" with the kind of life we believe we are owed. Osteen believes in this divine debt so much that he says this about our encounters with suffering: "God is going to balance your books. Payback is coming. . . . That attitude of faith is what allows God to pay you back for what you're owed."[27] As rebels and sinners, we have

---

26. Joel Osteen, *Think Better, Live Better: A Victorious Life Begins in Your Mind* (New York: FaithWords, 2016), 167; italics original.

27. Joel Osteen, *Blessed in the Darkness: How All Things Are Working for Your Good* (New York: FaithWords, 2017), 163–64.

forfeited God's good blessings and temporarily experience his kindness through the delay of his wrath and judgment (common grace). Yet, as his children saved through Christ, we have *privileges* afforded by God's saving grace, but not rights. Like Paul, we have laid down our rights that our boasting might be in the gospel, not our just deserts (1 Cor. 9:12–17). This way of thinking about God's blessing and creation may use similar language to what I have described earlier, but the theological posture of these two positions is fundamentally different.

Another great danger presented in this understanding of God's blessing is that it ignores the context of the biblical story. There are fundamental differences in the way that Osteen talks about blessing and the way I describe it here, and this difference is largely due to the lack of human rebellion and sin in his theological vision. The idea that human beings have the right to be blessed and God owes us good gifts not only misunderstands Genesis 1 and 2, but it completely ignores the reality of Genesis 3.

Humanity Rebels and Is Cursed

The sin of our first parents recorded in Genesis 3 is a direct attack on the moral arbiter of the universe. God determined what was "good" and "evil" for his creatures from the very beginning, but in Genesis 3 the man and woman decide for themselves what is good and evil, despite God declaring otherwise. The curse that ensues this act of rebellion is directly tied to God's blessing and purpose for his creatures. The order of the curse is reversed from the order in which we are introduced to each character in the creation narrative—man, woman, serpent. The implication is that the divine curse is a reversal of the creation blessing unfolding up until this point. The curse affects our ability to experience fullness of life and so also our ability to live in God's presence in the garden.

The presence of the two trees and the pursuit of knowledge in Genesis 3 reveal that this narrative is not just about the blunt, unthinking response of a rebel, but also the illicit pursuit of divine wisdom and knowledge. The Old Testament closely links the themes of wisdom, creation, and the fear of the Lord in portraying what it means to live the good life as God's people (Pss. 104:24; 111:10; Prov. 3:13–18; 8:22–36). "Whoever finds me finds life / and obtains favor from the LORD," Wisdom says in Proverbs 8:35. In their pursuit of knowledge and wisdom separate from God's revealed will, the man and woman walked away from the blessed life experienced by those who fear the Lord and keep his commandments (Deut. 13:4; Eccl. 12:13). Conversely, the one who fears the Lord is said to walk in wisdom. "The Old Testament knows a wisdom . . . that grows out of God's power to bless, and therefore . . . has a direct relationship to God's activity and work."[28] Ironically, because the man and woman did not walk in wisdom and fear God (that is, honor and revere his word and person), they ended up hiding behind the trees, now afraid of God!

HUMAN REBELLION THREATENS LIFE

The first reference in the Bible to the end of human life comes in the command of Genesis 2:16–17: "You may surely eat of every tree of the garden, but of the tree of the knowledge of good and evil you shall not eat, for in the day that you eat of it you shall surely die." These words are called into question when the serpent enigmatically emerges in Genesis 3, provoking the woman to evaluate the reliability of God's word. The serpent tells the woman that if she takes the fruit she "will not surely die," and she "will be like God, knowing good and evil" (3:4–5). When the woman and the man rebelled against God's

---

28. Westermann, *Blessing in the Bible*, 39. Note that Abraham demonstrates that he feared the Lord in Gen. 22 when he obediently offers up Isaac.

command and took the fruit and ate, as the serpent had stated, their eyes were opened to see the world differently. But not in a way that was good for them. From this point on, they would indeed know good *and evil*. The promised punishment of death in 2:17 would now render all humanity spiritually dead, physically mortal, expelled from God's presence.

Despite the serpent's alluring words, the man and the woman would die. As the chapter unfolds, God reveals the rebellious deed and pronounces a curse on the serpent and the ground. While the man and woman receive punishments from the Lord, the text does not explicitly say that they are cursed. The consequences of rebellion affect the woman's ability to fulfill the cultural mandate in 1:28 by introducing pain to the act of childbirth. This is not an arbitrary punishment but one that is directly tied to the woman's role in carrying out God's plan for humanity. The woman would still be able to bring forth life (see Gen. 4:1), but it would not be easy. Similarly, the man's punishment is directly tied to the cursing of the ground. He is commissioned to work and keep the ground, and from this point on the ground will fight back until it finally wins and swallows him up.

Scholars debate whether human mortality is introduced in Genesis 3:19 or whether human nature was always mortal but sustained by access to the tree of life (see 3:22). Regardless, by the end of chapter 3, the net result is the same—human beings will all experience physical death. In addition, the immediate response of the man and woman hiding from the Lord indicates that their act of rebellion did not just affect their material destiny but also their spiritual union with their Creator. Robin Routledge notes in his *Old Testament Theology*, "In the OT, physical death also has a spiritual dimension: it brings relationship with God to an end. . . . The real threat and real punishment here is expulsion from the garden, and with it exclusion from the blessings of being in God's presence."[29] Borrowing Paul's imagery from Ephesians 2:1, humanity—now separated from their Creator—would also experience a spiritual death due to their sin.

HUMAN REBELLION PRODUCES SEPARATION

The narrative of Genesis 3 portrays the creation design unraveling.[30] Humanity loses access to the tree of life and the giver of life. In response to their newly corrupt state, God drives them out of the garden lest they eat of the tree of life and stay estranged from God and one another. The man will no longer work the garden in Eden, but he is sent to work the ground from which he came. The couple is driven out to the east of the garden, and the Lord places a cherubim with a flaming sword to guard access to the garden.

Interestingly, this tragic picture will serve almost as a narrative blueprint for the arrangement of the tabernacle and temple. Both structures were entered from the east, both had blue and purple curtains with images of cherubim separating humanity from God's presence in the Holy of Holies, and both structures had garden-like carvings and characteristics reminiscent of God dwelling with his people in Eden. The reality is the same in all three scenarios—because of mankind's rebellion against God, God's people were no longer able to live in his presence.

The curses that followed the fall of humanity create a tension that permeates the Scriptures. What is going to happen to humanity now that the good design is distorted? What will God do with these conniving, self-serving creatures who rebelled against him? Will death and curse or blessing and life be the dominant story of the world? These are the questions thrown upon us as we read the first

---

29. Routledge, *Old Testament Theology*, 152.
30. T. D. Alexander, *From Paradise to Promised Land: An Introduction to the Pentateuch* (Grand Rapids, MI: Baker, 2002), 117.

three chapters of Genesis. John Walton notes, "The text has already established the blessing as the climax of chapter 1 and the objective of chapter 2. Aside from the idea of the blessing as the author's main theme, it stands to reason that having sinned and broken their relationship with God, the natural question is: Is the blessing of chapter 1 still intact?"[31] In fact, the rest of the biblical story is God's progressive revelation answering these initial questions. And the first answer to the question—What is God going to do with humanity now?—is also revealed in Genesis 3.

Blessing, Offspring, and Life

The effects of the fall recorded in Genesis 3 continue to plague humanity to this day. However, we don't even make it out of the chapter before we see God return to his ultimate commitment to blessing and life. As God is cursing the serpent, he speaks this important promise in Genesis 3:15: "I will put enmity [that is, hostility] between you and the woman, / and between your offspring and her offspring; / he shall bruise your head, / and you shall bruise his heel." The word translated "offspring" is also the Hebrew word for "seed," and the implications are that the seed of the woman is going to have a profound role in crushing the head of the serpent.

The seed promise of Genesis 3:15 is the initial bubbling of a thematic spring that will eventually widen to a prominent stream flowing throughout the Old Testament—God's blessing the world will be mediated by a chosen seed.[32] However, that chosen seed can emerge only because—despite her transgression—Eve will continue to function as the "mother of all living" (3:20), establishing two different lines through her sons Cain and Seth. The

---

31. John H. Walton, *Genesis*, NIV Application Commentary (Grand Rapids, MI: Zondervan, 2001), 238.

32. Alexander, *From Paradise to Promised Land*, 103–13.

promise of Genesis 3:15 requires that humanity continue through child-bearing; from one of those lines, a son will arise to crush the head of the serpent. Despite the fall and subsequent curses, God's plan to bless will move forward through the birth and life of his people.

2

Blessing the World through Abraham's Family

A Universal Family

With the rise of digital cataloging, researching family history has never been easier. Simply enter in a few facts your grandmother once told you, and you too can learn that you are descended from some ancient strain of aristocracy—something you were always suspicious of but never had the data to prove! Family history is important to our understanding of identity because we are all born into a story in progress.

"These Generations" and God's Plan to Bless

In the times of the biblical writers, people tracked family histories, major family events, and even the rise of leaders and kings, with genealogies. We see this in Genesis through an important little phrase woven throughout the book: "These are the generations." This phrase occurs eleven times in the book, with ten of these references serving as significant transitional headings.[1] The vehicle and sign of God's blessing is the continuing generations of humanity—that is, a seed.[2]

However, the ever-shortening lifespan revealed through the genealogies of Genesis 1–11 is also a continual reminder of the spread and consequence of human sin and rebellion. The progression of "these generations" in Genesis 1–11 is an indicator of the mortality of humanity and the divine commitment to continue to bless it to fill the earth. While we might not see the continuation of human life on earth as a profound divine blessing, the flood clearly teaches that life is a divine gift not to be presumed upon or taken lightly (see Gen. 9:4–5). Aside from the reality of divine blessing and human mortality, we also see a narrowing effect in the generational accounts that transitions us from seeing God's people as a universal phenomenon to a single family in Genesis 12. As Jason DeRouchie writes:

> The book of Genesis is framed in the context of divine blessing, wherein the divine image-bearers were commissioned to reflect, resemble, and represent God on a global scale, all through radical God-glorifying dependence (Gen 1:26–28). When viewed through this worldview-shaping prefatory lens, the ten *toledot* units in the rest of the book appear to clarify how the original *blessing-commission* was carried forward, rejected, and preserved, and how it would ultimately be realized in this fallen world.[3]

In Genesis 2–11 the generational genealogies are brought together with the undulating narrative pattern of grace-sin-punishment-

---

1. Gen. 2:4; 5:1; 6:9; 10:1; 11:10, 27; 25:12, 19; 36:1; 37:2. See Jason S. DeRouchie, "The Blessing-Commission, the Promised Offspring, and the *Toledot* Structure of Genesis," *Journal of the Evangelical Theological Society* 56, no. 2 (2013): 222–29.

2. David J. A. Clines, "Theme in Genesis 1–11," *Catholic Biblical Quarterly* 38, no. 4 (1976): 491. Clines also notes that the ever-shortening lifespan of individuals mentioned in the Genesis genealogies is an indicator of the encroaching mortality that accompanies humanity's sinful state.

3. DeRouchie, "The Blessing-Commission," 244.

grace. A quick look the stories of Adam and Eve, Cain and Abel, the "sons of God" and the flood, Noah and Ham, and the Tower of Babel reveals a striking pattern: (1) God graciously blesses humanity with life in his world, (2) the people spurn God's grace and created order, (3) punishment ensues, (4) yet God continues his program to bless the world through humanity.

For example, God benevolently grants Eve two sons, Cain and Abel. However, the one seed (Cain) rises up in hostility against the other seed (Abel) and murders him, despite the Lord's warning and instruction to rule over sin. Cain too is cursed by God because of his sin (Gen. 4:11–12). Cain's severed relationships with the created world, his fellow humans, and most importantly God are so affected that he cries: "My punishment is greater than I can bear. Behold, you have driven me today away from the ground, and from your face I shall be hidden" (4:13–14). The broken and cursed life Cain is to experience is a negative reflection of the life he was intended to live with God in his good world. However, in a subsequent act of grace, God provides a promise of protection and provision for Cain's life. Recognizing this divine pattern, David Clines aptly summarizes the theme of Genesis 1–11 this way: "No matter how drastic man's sin becomes, destroying what God has made good and bringing the world to the brink of uncreation, God's grace never fails to deliver man from the consequences of his sin. Even when man responds to a fresh start with the old pattern of sin, God's commitment to his world stands firm, and sinful man experiences the favor of God as well as his righteous judgment."[4]

Noah as the New Adam

The reality of the commingling of human sin and divine blessing continues to emerge from the narratives of Genesis 4–11. After the

---

4. Clines, "Theme in Genesis 1–11," 502.

tragedy of Abel, God gave Eve another son named Seth, and the "generations of Adam" in 5:1 is the line of Seth, not Cain. Despite the curse of Cain, human life will continue. Tragically, however, the line of Seth was not impervious to the stain of sin any more than Cain, and in 6:5 we read that "the LORD saw that the wickedness of man was great in the earth, and that every intention of the thoughts of his heart was only evil continually." And so, despite God's grief over the corruption of his good creation, he cleansed his world, preserving his blessing through the "generations of Noah" (6:9).

Amid the darkness and corruption of the pre-flood world, Noah's righteousness must have stood out (Gen. 6:9); however, the previous verse tells us that it was because of God's grace, or "favor," that he and his family would be spared from the global punishment. In Genesis 6:18, God establishes the first explicit covenant recorded in Scripture, and this covenant is ratified later in 9:9–11. Extending his covenant promises to Noah and his descendants, God graciously preserves the seed of the woman, while also bringing humanity and living creatures into renewed relationship with the Lord, despite God's decision to make an "end to all flesh" (6:13).

As the waters rise and submerge the world God created, everything returns once again to the chaotic state described in Genesis 1:2. Joseph Blenkinsopp has used the phrase "creation-un-creation-re-creation" to summarize the development of the story from creation to the flood and beyond.[5] As an act of "uncreation," the flood also stands as a reversal of God's blessing at creation. So, if the flood is the divine reset on creation, then Noah functions as Adam 2.0. In fact, there are several reasons to view Noah as a second Adam. First, the "be fruitful and multiply" phrase is restated three separate times in this account (8:17; 9:1, 7), presenting Noah, his

5. Joseph Blenkinsopp, *Creation, Un-Creation, Re-Creation: A Discursive Commentary on Genesis 1–11* (New York: T&T Clark International, 2011).

family, and the living creatures with the same creational program of procreation. The command in 9:1 is prefaced by the phrase "And God blessed," identifying the command/blessing as the same blessing declared over humanity in 1:28. Second, Adam and Noah are both presented as men who cultivate the ground. Third, while the Hebrew word for "curse" is different, God states that he will "never again curse the ground because of [mankind]" (Gen. 8:21; cf. 3:17). Fourth, Genesis 9 presents Noah and his children as continuing to possess dominion and authority over the living creatures of the earth (Gen. 9:2–3). And finally, lest the flood tempt people to think mankind is of little value, God confirms in 9:6 that humanity still bears his image and that image shall not be removed without due recompense. So, in the wake of the tragic flood, the themes of blessing, creation (or re-creation), and covenant are woven together to present a hopeful context for covenant life in relationship with God.

Unfortunately, we quickly learn that sin is not simply a quantitative problem perpetuated by the masses—it is an intrinsic disordering in the human heart. The themes of blessing and curse are once again closely found in later verses of Genesis 9. God graciously delivers Noah and his family and blesses them to be fruitful and fill the earth, yet the shadows quickly darken. Carol Kaminski has noted that the language of spreading out in Genesis 9:19 presents an ominous foreshadowing of the punishment and scattering at Babel.[6] In the final scene of Genesis 9, Noah became drunk and was lying naked in his tent when his son Ham "saw the nakedness of his father and told his two brothers outside" (9:22). It is unclear exactly what this means, but whether Ham simply saw his father unclothed or

---

6. Carol M. Kaminski, *From Noah to Israel: Realization of the Primaeval Blessing after the Flood*, Library of Hebrew Bible/Old Testament Studies 413 (New York: T&T Clark International, 2004), 41. See also T. D. Alexander, *From Paradise to Promised Land: An Introduction to the Pentateuch* (Grand Rapids, MI: Baker, 2002), 119.

there was some sexual impropriety,[7] the exposure of Noah's naked-ness and subsequent curse are eerily reminiscent of Genesis 3.[8]

Once Noah awoke from his drunken sleep, he made a declaration over his sons: a curse over Canaan (the descendent of Ham and historic foe of the people of Israel) and a word of blessing over his other sons, especially Shem.

> "Cursed be Canaan;
>> a servant of servants shall he be to his brothers."

He also said,

> "Blessed be the LORD, the God of Shem;
>> and let Canaan be his servant.
> May God enlarge Japheth,
>> and let him dwell in the tents of Shem,
>> and let Canaan be his servant." (Gen. 9:25–27)

As many commentators have noted, the words of Noah in this passage should not be identified with the divine voice speaking blessings and curses earlier in the book. The grammar and context of Noah's pronouncement make it best understood as an invocation, or request, that God curse and bless accordingly—not a prophetic declaration.[9] The curse against Canaan reveals the authoritative nature found in divine blessing. According to Noah's words, for the descendants of Ham and Canaan to be cursed, they would live lives of undesired servitude.

---

7. The exact details of the account are difficult to discern, but based on Lev. 18:7–8, it is possible that the impropriety is maternal incest, with Canaan being the result.

8. Blenkinsopp, *Creation, Un-Creation, Re-Creation*, 154.

9. See Kenneth A. Mathews, *Genesis 1–11:26*, New American Commentary 1A (Nashville, TN: Broadman & Holman, 1996), 422; Nahum Sarna, *Genesis*, JPS Torah Commentary (Philadelphia: Jewish Publication Society, 1989), 66; Victor P. Hamilton, *The Book of Genesis, Chapters 1–17*, New International Commentary on the Old Testament (Grand Rapids, MI: Eerdmans, 1990), 324.

Interestingly, the word *blessed* used in Genesis 9:26 is directed toward God, instead of Shem or Japheth, as one might expect. However, the content of Noah's words reveals "the patriarch's recognition that what blessing comes to Shem is the Lord's doing."[10] The formula uttered by Noah, "Blessed be the LORD," is a common form of praise (Gen. 14:20; 24:27; Ex. 18:10), and it is the first time in Scripture the divine name (YHWH) is associated with a specific people. "The intention of this blessing seems to be clearly attached to the possession of the divine name Yahweh itself,"[11] and demonstrates the relationship that exists between YHWH and Shem. The word spoken on behalf of Japheth is a plea that God would open or "enlarge" his line, but even with this expansion, Japheth would still dwell within the tents of Shem. Noah's final words in the Bible ask God to abide with his son Shem, allow for fraternal peace (as opposed to Cain and Abel), and place him in a position of authority over his brothers.

It is not entirely clear why Canaan, the son of Ham, is cursed instead of Ham himself. Nonetheless, in this moment of family crisis, two family lines emerge from the new humanity established in Noah—one cursed (Canaan) and one blessed (Shem). The genealogies that follow in chapters 10 and 11 continue the conflicting-seed drama that was pronounced in Genesis 3:15, while also foreshadowing the future conflict between the peoples dwelling in Canaan and the descendants of Shem, Abram's offspring. And despite humanity's new strategy to make a great name for themselves at the Tower of Babel, God would establish a great name among humanity and make sure that all the families of the earth experience his blessing. But he would do it through one family.

---

10. Mathews, *Genesis 1–11:26*, 423.

11. William J. Dumbrell, *Covenant and Creation: A Theology of Old Testament Covenants* (Nashville, TN: Thomas Nelson, 1984), 63.

Abraham's Family

A Land, a People, and God's Blessing (Genesis 12:1–3)

The focus of God's people, his relationship to them, and his desire to bless the world shift dramatically in Genesis 12. Like a river narrowing before a cascade, the genealogies of Genesis 1–11 carry us to a precipice of divine activity where the themes of blessing, seed, and land come pouring over. In Genesis 11:27 we are introduced to a certain Mesopotamian man named Terah, who had three sons[12] and traveled westward with one of his sons and grandson to the fertile plains of Haran. And it is here, roughly four hundred miles north of the land of Canaan, that Terah's son Abram (later to become Abraham) received his commissioning and promise of blessing from God. We know nothing about Abram that would make him a more likely candidate for blessing than others, so the abrupt call of God in 12:1–3 reflects nothing other than God's sovereign election of Abram's line.[13]

> Now the LORD said to Abram, "Go from your country and your kindred and your father's house to the land that I will show you. And I will make of you a great nation, and *I will bless* you and make your name great, so that you will *be a blessing. I will bless* those who *bless* you, and him who dishonors you I will curse, and in you all the families of the earth *shall be blessed.*"[14]

---

12. Peter Gentry and Stephen Wellum highlight the three-son pattern observed from Adam (Cain, Abel, and Seth) to Noah (Shem, Ham, and Japheth) to Terah (Abram, Nahor, and Haran), possibly inciting Abram's comparison with Adam and Noah. See Peter J. Gentry and Stephen J. Wellum, *Kingdom through Covenant: A Biblical-Theological Understanding of the Covenants* (Wheaton, IL: Crossway, 2012), 224.

13. Graeme Goldsworthy, *According to Plan: The Unfolding Revelation of God in the Bible* (Downers Grove, IL: IVP, 1991), 122.

14. For a defense of the passive "shall be blessed," see Keith N. Grüneberg, *Abraham, Blessing and the Nations: A Philological and Exegetical Study of Genesis 12:3 in Its Narrative Context*, Beihefte zur Zeitschrift für die alttestamentliche Wissenschaft 332 (Berlin: De Gruyter, 2003), 65–66.

In Genesis 3–11, the Hebrew word for *curse* is found in five places, and the fivefold repetition of blessing in these verses clearly indicates that the promise given to Abram is to serve as the divine corrective to the unshakable sin and curse that has plagued humanity up until this point.[15] It is as if these verses in Genesis 12 are answering the anticipated post-Babel question: "What now? What is going to happen to these Cain-like people wandering the world and God's plan to bless the world?" In short, God will bless the world through Abram and his offspring. Abram is to be the embodiment of God's blessing, and as such, two factors follow: (1) those who respond rightly to Abram and his line receive God's blessing, and (2) Abram and his progeny are to mediate that blessing to the world.

The passage has a relatively clear structure that begins with a command to "go," followed by the promise of a land, a national heritage, a great name, protection, and blessing. Then a second command to "be a blessing" is followed by the promises of divine favor and universal blessing.[16] If Abram is going to experience the fullness of life in God's presence, he must submit to the sovereign rule of God over his life—a lesson already illustrated in the sad events of Genesis 3–4.[17] Faith-driven obedience to the word of God is inseparably tied to the reality of divine blessing throughout the Scriptures. Note, however, that Abram's obedience does not earn God's blessing, but instead flows out of a faith in the revealed promises of God. Abram trusted that God would do what he said. Carol Kaminski writes, "Since the primaeval blessing has been changed into a divine *promise,* there is also the suggestion that the behavior of the patriarchs

15. Kenneth A. Mathews, *Genesis 11:27–50:26*, New American Commentary 1B (Nashville, TN: Broadman & Holman, 2005), 105.

16. Paul R. Williamson, *Sealed with an Oath: Covenant in God's Unfolding Purpose*, New Studies in Biblical Theology 23 (Downers Grove, IL: IVP, 2007), 82–84.

17. Allen P. Ross, *Creation & Blessing: A Guide to the Study and Exposition of Genesis* (Grand Rapids, MI: Baker, 1998), 262–63.

cannot jeopardize its realization."[18] Abram's obedience was the means God employed to bring about his plan to bless the world, but Abram's faith was not perfect, as we see in the fears and failures of his life.[19] In fact, the patriarchal narratives of Abraham and Jacob seem to emphasize that God's commitment to bless his people will always overcome threats and failures.[20]

The promise of blessing begins with God instructing Abram to go to a new land, a land that would be explicitly promised to him in Genesis 12:7. However, despite leaving his father's house, there is no concern that Abram will be traveling alone. Abram must respond in obedience and travel to a foreign land, but God is the one who is in control of Abram's journey. Divine blessing—while often including notions such as fertility, possessions, success, and authority—must always be understood within the framework of one's relationships to God and others.[21] With every first-person pronoun in this passage, we see God's promise to be actively present in Abraham's life: leading, showing, making, cursing, and blessing. Given the necessary journey, there is little doubt that Abraham's blessing and great name would include divine provision and favor throughout his sojourning. God is the sovereign guarantor of the promise, and he will accomplish it.

In response to the curse of Genesis 3, God drove Adam and Eve out of his garden and away from his presence, yet in the Abrahamic program of blessing God is once again bringing his people to his land, where he will dwell with them. "God's purpose in issuing the patriarchal blessing promises is to call the patriarchs into a close re-

---

18. Kaminski, *From Noah to Israel*, 107.

19. Paul's emphasis on Abraham's life was not Abraham's moral perfection but his faith in God's promises. See David Lincicum, "Genesis in Paul," in *Genesis in the New Testament*, ed. Maarten J. J. Menken and Steve Moyise, Library of New Testament Studies 466 (New York: Bloomsbury T&T Clark, 2012), 106–12.

20. Hamilton, *Genesis 1–17*, 43.

21. Christopher J. H. Wright, *The Mission of God: Unlocking the Bible's Grand Narrative* (Downers Grove, IL: IVP Academic, 2006), 209–10.

lationship with himself."[22] The predominant Promised Land theme that runs throughout the Old Testament finds its theological source in Eden, not Canaan. Abram and his descendants were to experience the blessed life of 12:2–3 in God's place with God. God spoke with Adam and gave him a garden. God spoke with Noah and gave him a newly re-created world. And God spoke with Abram and gave him a promised land.

God's promise is not just a place for Abram to tie up his camels! He is leading Abram to a land where he will be blessed with children, and his family line will become a great nation. While it is not until Genesis 17 that we see the blessing and covenant explicitly extended to Abram's offspring, the promise to make him into a great nation necessitates the existence of children. The fulfillment of God's promised blessing will be through the continuation of Abram's line by means of a seed. But we have already been tipped off to know that there is a subtle tension in the promise, because Genesis 11:30 makes it explicitly clear that "Sarai was barren; she had no child." Her barrenness—like the flood—points to a reversal of God's planned blessing-initiative at creation (Gen. 1:26–28). Knowing these circumstances, we are immediately met with a sense of wonder and a bit of tension in God's promising to make Abram a great nation. But God's intentions to bless the world through Abram and Sarai will soon be revealed to the patriarch as clearly as the stars shining in the darkness.

We would be mistaken to see God's blessing in these verses as a promise for Abram alone.[23] As we have seen already, God's desire to bless Abram and his family is rooted in his initial desire to bless the world, and this is reiterated in Genesis 12:3 by all the "families of the earth" being blessed in Abram. This reference to the "earth" or

---

22. Christopher W. Mitchell, *The Meaning of BRK "To Bless" in the Old Testament*, SBL Dissertation Series 95 (Atlanta: Scholars, 1987), 29.

23. Dumbrell, *Covenant and Creation*, 74.

"ground" directs our attention to the cursed ground in Genesis 3:17 (same word!) and God's promise to never curse the ground again in 8:21. The global curse has met its covenantal match of blessing. The universal scope of Genesis 1–11 is narrowed down to a single man and his wife, but from this unlikely couple God will accomplish his original plans of blessing. Abram's role in this universal plan is highlighted in Genesis 18:18 when the Lord refuses to keep his plan from him because he "surely [shall] become a great and mighty nation, and all the nations of the earth shall be blessed in him." And again, in response to his obedience to offer up his son Isaac, the angel of the Lord states that "in your offspring shall all the nations of the earth be blessed" (Gen. 22:18).

The immediate fulfillment of the divine promise is manifested in Abram's children, and eventually the nation of Israel. However, we should not overlook this missional component of the promise. "Israel as a nation, as a symbol of divine rule manifested within a political framework, was intended itself to be an image of the shape of *final* world government, a symbol pointing beyond itself to the reality yet to be."[24] From this future-oriented vision of God's transnational reign over the families of the earth, the blessing of Abram extends through faith in the "seed," who is Christ (Gal. 3:16). Paul exposes the missional force of Genesis 12 when he says in Galatians 3:8–9, "And the Scripture, foreseeing that God would justify the Gentiles by faith, preached the gospel beforehand to Abraham, saying, 'In you shall all the nations be blessed.' So then, those who are of faith are blessed along with Abraham, the man of faith." While not yet fully realized, the latent good news of global blessing—the fullness of life in the presence of God—was proclaimed in this brief, but profound, promise to Abram.

---

24. Dumbrell, *Covenant and Creation*, 73.

In the subsequent chapters of Genesis, God's blessing upon Abram comes into focus. Despite the fear and deception in Egypt that led Abram to give his wife to Pharaoh, God brings plagues upon Pharaoh, and Abram leaves Egypt under nothing less than divine protection. The focus on the division of land between Lot and Abram revisits the promise of 12:1. In Genesis 14, Abram rescues his nephew Lot by conquering a hoard of Canaanite kings and, consequently, he receives a blessing from Melchizedek in 14:19–20: "And he blessed him and said, 'Blessed be Abram by God Most High, / Possessor of heaven and earth; / and blessed be God Most High, / who has delivered your enemies into your hand!'" God is granting Abram protection, favor in the eyes of outsiders, and victory over his enemies as he sojourns in the land of Canaan. In fact, the royal themes of these two chapters depict Abram possessing a "great name" in the ancient world. Bill Arnold writes, "To have a great name given to one by God in the Hebrew Scriptures is to be viewed as a royal figure (2 Sam. 7:9)."[25] However, while Abram's wealth, protection, and military victory might be tied to the notion of his having a great name, land and a future offspring were a major focus of God's promise in 12:1–3. So, when God appears to Abram again in chapter 15, we see that he needs some divine reassurance that the Lord is committed to his original plan to bless the world through his family.

A Promise Sealed and a Covenant Cut (Genesis 15)

If the rise of the fast food culture has taught us anything, it is that people are willing to make some serious compromises in order to avoid waiting. The fact is we all hate waiting, especially when we have been assured that something wonderful is coming but we just don't

25. Bill T. Arnold, *Genesis* (Cambridge: Cambridge University Press, 2009), 132.

know when. In Genesis 15, Abram is clearly concerned about how God's promise is going to work out, given his current circumstances. However, it is with Abram's psalm-like laments—"Oh Lord GOD, what will you give me?" and "Oh Lord GOD, how am I to know?"—that God seals his promise in 12:1–3 with a unilateral (one-sided) covenant.

Genesis 15 is easily divided into two sections, each featuring an opening word from the Lord, a reply from Abram asking for reassurance, and then a divine answer. In the first interaction, the problem is that of offspring. God tells Abram, "Fear not, Abram, I am your shield; your reward shall be very great" (15:1). But Abram doesn't understand, because a member of his household will inherit all that is his—and he has no son. In reply, God explains to Abram that (1) he will have a son from his own body, a singular offspring that will carry along the promise of blessing, and (2) this offspring (lit. "seed") would become as numerous as the stars of the sky. Then we are told " [Abram] believed the LORD, and he counted it to him as righteousness" (15:6). Abram believed in the promise that God would provide a seed through Abram's own body to accomplish God's plan to bless his line, and eventually the world. As we will see, this promise of offspring to Abram starts to take shape in the generations that immediately follow, eventually giving rise to the nation of Israel. But these words in Genesis 15:6 have a significant role in the New Testament's understanding of faith, blessing, and righteousness.

I have never seen Genesis 15:6 held up in the stands of a sporting event, but for the apostle Paul, this text was pivotal in understanding God's work of redemption. In Romans 4 Paul unpacks the significance of Abram's faith in the promise of God for an offspring. However, Paul's focus is on contrasting righteousness through faith instead of works, and for Paul, this is not divorced from the idea of God's blessing. In the middle of Romans 4, he comments on and quotes from Psalm 32:1–2: "David also speaks of the blessing of the one to whom God counts righteousness apart from works: 'Blessed are those whose lawless deeds are forgiven, / and whose sins are covered; / blessed is the man against whom the Lord will not count his sin'" (Rom. 4:6–8). As Paul reflects on the faith of Abram in Genesis 15, he sees the profound relationship between Abram's faith in the promise of God and the sin-covering righteousness accounted to him for that faith. For Paul, Abram's blessing was not simply to get children; it was to get God! The blessing was not stuff but status—being declared righteous by God (Rom. 4:24). And this was not simply for himself—"The purpose was to make him the father of all who believe" (Rom. 4:11).

The second part of Genesis 15 turns from the starry-sky promise of offspring to an animal-cutting covenant dealing with the land. God speaks to Abram a second time, telling him, "I am the LORD who brought you out from Ur of the Chaldeans to give you this land to possess" (15:7), which prompts Abram's question, "How am I to know that I shall possess it?" (15:8). The answer that God provides is quite clear within its cultural context, but it seems a bit strange to us. God tells Abram to get several animals, cut them in half, and set the halves across from each other. God is giving Abram proof that he will keep his promise—covenantal proof. He is setting up the scene for a covenant, where covenant members would pass between the pieces of the animals, indicating that if a person breaks the covenant, they shall be liable to the same picture of death on either side of them (see Jer. 34:18–20).[26] A deep sleep comes over Abram, and the Lord tells him emphatically to "know for certain" that his offspring (again, lit. "seed") will be sojourners in Egypt but they will come back to possess this land after he has brought judgments upon the

---

26. See Gentry and Wellum, *Kingdom through Covenant*, 251–56.

nation oppressing them. Then we are told: "When the sun had gone down and it was dark, behold, a smoking fire pot and a flaming torch passed between these pieces. On that day the LORD made a covenant with Abram, saying, 'To your offspring I give this land . . .'" (15:17–18). What was Abram's proof that God was going to keep his promise concerning the land? The smoking fire pot and flaming torch (see Ex. 13:21; 19:18) indicate that God answered Abram's question with a unilateral, one-sided covenant, where he alone passed through the pieces of the animals. God promises to Abram that his covenant people would have a land—a place where they would experience his blessing.

Just as we saw in Genesis 1–3, the fullness of life in the presence of God requires a living people and place to dwell with God. The covenants with Noah and Abram both reveal how God is working out his blessing initiative in a sinful world. In Genesis 9 God universally covenants with humanity and the living creatures never to bring destruction over all the earth again. While this covenant continues, Genesis 15 shows that God's plan to bless the world is universal in scope ("all the families of the earth") but not number.

THE COVENANT DEVELOPED AND CONFIRMED (GENESIS 17 AND 21)

God's covenant with Abram is developed further in Genesis 17, reaching its fullest form. After Abram's illicit attempt to produce an heir with Hagar in chapter 16, God comes to Abram again and confirms his promise of offspring. This confirmation is not simply a restatement of things, however. Abram's and Sarai's names are changed, we are informed that nations and kings will come from them, God's covenant is formally established with the offspring and not just Abraham, the covenant is called "an everlasting covenant," and God initiates circumcision as the sign of the covenant, to name a few of the differences.[27]

The language of "multiply" and "exceedingly fruitful" in these texts is reminiscent of the cultural mandate given in Genesis 1:26–28, and here we see the covenantal and creational impulse "to bless" forged together. God's plan has always been global blessing, and it continues to be global even within the context of the Abrahamic covenant. While humanity will continue to "be fruitful and multiply," having dominion over created animals, there is a relational and covenantal aspect to experience God's blessing that will be unique for his chosen people (Gen. 17:7). Already in the Abrahamic covenant we are seeing a separation between mere biological life and fertility and life lived according to God's good design—rightly relating to God, others, and his creation. God will bless Ishmael, multiply him, make him fruitful, and even make him into a great nation (17:20), but he will only establish his covenant through Isaac. The rite of circumcision will be the visible sign of this new blessed human line throughout the rest of the Old Testament.

In Genesis 17 the patriarch's name is changed to Abraham, which alludes to his new role as "father of a multitude of nations." During a time when the blessings were still future promises, "the new names were tangible benefits that the patriarchs received immediately to help assure them of God's future blessings."[28] Abram's embrace of his new self-identity as "Abraham" was confirmation for himself and others, that *he did* have a new role to play in God's redemptive plan for the nations and that he did in fact *believe* in the promise of God's blessing and a future offspring. We also find out that Sarah had a role to play as well. She too is promised the divine blessing that

---

27. See Gordon Wenham, *Genesis 16–50*, Word Biblical Commentary 2 (Nashville, TN: Thomas Nelson, 2000), 16–19.

28. Mitchell, *The Meaning of BRK*, 35.

will produce a son, and moreover, she will be the mother of kings and nations. In Genesis 17 the portrait of Abraham's family as having royal status in God's divine plan to bless is brought to the fore. God's blessing will produce kings, and his blessing will be mediated through them.

Abraham's new role in redemptive history is confirmed with a divine oath in Genesis 22. Having received the gut-wrenching command to offer up his son Isaac on the mountain as a sacrifice, Abraham's obedience prompts a final oath confirming his role in God's plans of blessing: "By myself I have sworn, declares the LORD, because you have done this and have not withheld your son, your only son, I will surely bless you, and I will surely multiply your offspring as the stars of heaven and as the sand that is on the seashore. And your offspring shall possess the gate of his enemies, and in your offspring shall all the nations of the earth be blessed, because you have obeyed my voice" (22:16–18). As the writer of Hebrews asserts, God has provided the greatest assurance possible in swearing by himself that he will bless Abraham and his offspring (Heb. 6:13).

This text, more than any other in the story of Abraham, points to the connection between the patriarch's faith-driven obedience and the certainty of his blessing. Unlike our first parents in the garden, Abraham's obedience demonstrated that he feared God, believed in God's word, and secured blessing for his progeny instead of curses. As we saw earlier in Genesis 12 and 17, God gives commands to Abraham, and they often precede words of promise and blessing that follow. This should not give us pause or lead us to think that the covenant with Abraham is actually setting us up for a merit-based picture of divine blessing. First, the text never provides any reason as to why Abraham would have merited God's selection as the mediator of blessing to the world. He is simply and graciously called out by God to be blessed and to be blessing. Second, God's commitment to bless his world in Genesis 3–11 reveals that Abraham is his chosen means of blessing, but God's divine plans are not riding on Abraham's ability to make good choices (in fact, he often doesn't). Third, God's promises preceded the commands. Several of the commands found in the story of Abraham follow the divine promises revealed in Genesis 12:1–3 and Genesis 15, and this is significant for the apostle Paul. In fact, Paul bases his understanding of faith *versus* works on the chronological relationship between the promise revealed (Genesis 15) and the covenant sign of circumcision. Fourth, implicit within all the commands and promises given to Abraham is the basic duty of mankind—faith in God's words. Abraham's obedience and experience of God's blessing flowed directly from his faith. He did not earn God's favor or blessing, but instead believed that it had been promised to him, and then walked in that faith. The close of the Abraham story confirms that God kept his covenant promise, stating, "Now Abraham was old, well advanced in years. And the LORD had blessed Abraham in all things" (Gen. 24:1).

Blessing in the Families of Isaac and Jacob

God's covenant with Abraham and the consequent blessings are passed down to and through his sons in the remainder of the book of Genesis. In Genesis 17 God declared that his covenant would be upon the not-yet-conceived Isaac, and this is made explicit in 26:3–5: "Sojourn in this land, and I will be with you and will bless you, for to you and to your offspring I will give all these lands, and I will establish the oath that I swore to Abraham your father. I will multiply your offspring as the stars of heaven and will give to your offspring all these lands. And in your offspring all the nations of the earth shall be blessed, because Abraham obeyed my voice and kept my charge, my commandments, my statutes, and my laws." God's words to Isaac reiterate that his experience of covenant blessing will be experienced in relationship to the divine presence. When Isaac departs from the land of Abimelech, God reassures him, "Fear not, for *I am with you* and will bless you and multiply your offspring for my servant Abraham's sake" (26:24). In the words of blessing given to Isaac, a significant development is present. God's faithfulness to Isaac is not on account of *his* obedience, but on account of Abraham. God's promise to bless the world through Abraham demonstrated his commitment to his initial world-blessing agenda in Genesis 1:26–28, and his promise to Isaac reveals his commitment to his covenant promises to bless the world through Abraham.

God's presence in the sojourning of the patriarchs is foundational to their experience of prosperity, fertility, and wealth that they will come to know. The themes of land, offspring, and blessing persist through God's covenant promise to Isaac. The final sentence in Genesis 26:4 quotes Genesis 22:18—"in your offspring shall all the nations of the earth be blessed"—and ties Isaac's covenantal status to the oath given to Abraham in Genesis 22. As with Abraham, God kept his promise, and "the LORD blessed him, and the man became rich, and gained more and more until he became very wealthy. He had possessions of flocks and herds and many servants, so that the Philistines envied him" (26:12–14). However, we also know that Isaac was blessed with more than flocks. His wife, Rebekah, is blessed by her family so that she might "become thousands of ten thousands" and her "offspring possess the gate of those who hate him" (24:60). And, despite her barrenness, she bore two sons—Jacob and Esau.

Jacob is one of the more complex characters in the book of Genesis; the work of God in Jacob's life takes him from being an impetuous young trickster fleeing from his big brother to a flawed but faithful patriarch of a fledgling people. Consequently, Jacob's acquisition of blessing pushes against any neat, equation-like notions of blessing. Jacob's place of prominence over his brother was made known to Rebekah before he was born (Gen. 25:23), but it would be through trickery and deceit that he would come to be blessed by his father, Isaac. Walther Zimmerli rightly notes, "In the midst of all the human confusion and contriving that surrounds this story, what happened was what Yahweh, in accordance with his mysterious decision, wanted to happen."[29] When Jacob flees from his brother, God appears to him and relays a blessing very similar to the one he gave to Isaac—a promise of land, numerous offspring, and "in you and your offspring shall all the families of the earth be blessed" (28:14). We have come to expect these words as we have worked through the promise given to the patriarchs. With Jacob, there is also a pronounced sense of God's presence: "Behold, *I am with you* and will keep you wherever you go, and will bring you back to this land. For I will not leave you until I have done what I have promised you" (28:15). Throughout the life of Abraham, we see God's presence in Jacob's life overcoming threats to ensure his promise. Gordon Wenham writes of Jacob's return to meet Esau, "This story, like many in Genesis, illustrates God's sovereign protection of his chosen. Despite Jacob's tactlessness and self-seeking, God has kept his promise made at Bethel that he would be with Jacob and guard him wherever he went (28:15)."[30]

Just as Jacob's character is transformed through his dealings with the Lord, like his grandfather and grandmother, his name is also changed. However, in Genesis 32, the new name *is* the blessing. He was no longer the trickster, supplanter, and "heel" of his youth. Jacob would be called *Israel*—"because you have struggled with God, and with men you have succeeded."[31] When Jacob left the land of Canaan

29. Walther Zimmerli, *The Old Testament and the World*, trans. J. J. Scullion (London: SPCK, 1976), 28.

30. Wenham, *Genesis 16–50*, 282.

31. Victor P. Hamilton, *The Book of Genesis, Chapters 18–50*, New International Commentary on the Old Testament (Grand Rapids, MI: Eerdmans, 1995), 335.

fleeing from his brother, God met him and blessed him (28:13). James McKeown astutely comments on God's blessing given to Jacob as he comes back to Canaan:

> Now on his return, as he stands on the outskirts of the land with apprehension about meeting Esau, God blesses him once again (32:29). This incident shows that true blessing and possession of the promised land come, not by deception or strife, but from Yahweh himself. So far Jacob's whole life had been a continual struggle, and even his wives turn the natural act of giving birth into a struggle for supremacy. Now he must learn that true blessing is a gift of God.[32]

That true blessing would not only change Jacob's name, but also his gait. The wrestling match had left him with a permanent limp (Gen. 32:31). Jacob's life challenges our simplistic categories of "do good things and be blessed" or "you are blessed so nothing hurts." In Jacob's limp we see God's severe mercy going to great lengths to produce the transformation and blessing in our lives, but not always in the way we wanted. Jacob's blessing in this story is not the wealth and children he had previously acquired. "Outside expressions of blessing (offspring and wealth) have moved to the periphery of the narrative. At the heart of the blessing Jacob now receives lies a change in how Jacob can view himself, both in relationship with God and man."[33] Jesus also teaches his disciples of a commingling of suffering and a life of blessing in the Sermon on the Mount. And he would later reveal that, in a fallen world, the way to divine blessing always involves suffering (Luke 9:23–26; see Rom. 8:17).

---

32. James McKeown, *Genesis*, The Two Horizons Old Testament Commentary (Grand Rapids, MI: Eerdmans, 2008), 155.

33. Paul D. Vrolijk, *Jacob's Wealth: An Examination into the Nature and Role of Material Possessions in the Jacob-Cycle (Gen 25:19–35:29)*, Vetus Testamentum Supplement Series 146 (Leiden: Brill, 2011), 242.

In Genesis 35:11–12, Jacob is provided a final summary of his covenant status before the Lord: "I am God Almighty: be fruitful and multiply. A nation and a company of nations shall come from you, and kings shall come from your own body. The land that I gave to Abraham and Isaac I will give to you, and I will give the land to your offspring after you." The blessing reads like a covenantal quilt comprised of language from God's dealing with humanity throughout the book of Genesis. The theme of kingship once again emerges, linking the promise of progeny with that of dominion and rule for God's people.

As the book of Genesis ends, Jacob and his seed have escaped the blessing-threat of famine in Egypt and the nations have been blessed through the leadership of Jacob's seed Joseph (Gen. 47:10). Jacob then gathers all his sons together to proclaim "what shall happen" in the coming days (Gen. 49). The two longest and most significant blessings are given to Judah and Joseph. While we might expect the blessing of leadership and authority to extend to Joseph, it is given to Judah.[34] "The scepter shall not depart from Judah, / nor the ruler's staff from between his feet" (Gen. 49:10). These words direct our eyes forward to the king from the line of Judah—David, and the fulfillment of the patriarchal promise of a royal lineage.[35]

The final verses of the blessing of Joseph describe God's blessing plainly:

> By the God of your father who will help you,
> > by the Almighty who will bless you
> > with blessings of heaven above,

---

34. T. D. Alexander, "Messianic Ideology in Genesis," in *The Lord's Anointed: Interpretation of Old Testament Messianic Texts*, ed. P. E. Satterthwaite, R. S. Hess, and G. J. Wenham (Eugene, OR: Wipf & Stock, 1995), 34.

35. T. D. Alexander, *From Paradise to the Promised Land* (Grand Rapids, MI: Baker, 2002), 110–11, 127.

blessings of the deep that crouches beneath,

blessings of the breasts and of the womb.

The blessings of your father

are mighty beyond the blessings of my parents,

up to the bounties of the everlasting hills.

May they be on the head of Joseph,

and on the brow of him who was set apart from his

brothers. (Gen. 49:25–26)

If the words of Judah confirmed the blessing of a royal seed from Jacob's line, the blessing given to Joseph focuses on life in the Promised Land. The language points toward God's blessing of fertility for both land and people, and this language is echoed in Moses's blessing of Joseph before going into the land in Deuteronomy 33:13–17. The blessings of both Judah and Joseph draw upon previous promises given to Abraham, Isaac, and Jacob, but they also carry the storyline of blessing forward as we look toward God's reign over his people in the land he promised them. In the final verses of the book Joseph tells his brothers, "As for you, you meant evil against me, but God meant it for good, to bring it about that many people should be kept alive, as they are today" (Gen. 50:20). In many ways this verse not only summarizes God's work in and through the challenges of Joseph's life, but it also speaks to God's promise of blessing working itself out through the entire book of Genesis.

Conclusion

Examining the Bible's portrait of blessing in the lives of the patriarchs is a rewarding challenge. Throughout these stories we see God's unswerving commitment to his plan to bless his world, the faith of Abraham in the promises of God's blessing, and the Lord's relentless grace and long-suffering with Jacob. The concept of blessing is employed in multiple ways and often seems to be pointing toward material prosperity. In his outstanding work on wealth in the life of Jacob, Paul Vrolijk notes that in the Abraham stories, blessing is often seen as God's words and actions on behalf of his people.[36] However, in the Isaac and Jacob stories, blessing shifts to include notions of greeting (Gen. 24:31), acts of praise (24:48), paternal declarations (27:27–29), presents to others (33:11), and prosperity (26:12). This is not surprising. While God's actions with Abraham are not disconnected from the previous eleven chapters of Genesis, there is a certain newness to the program of blessing begun in his lifetime. Isaac and Jacob inherit the promise, and it is in their lives that we begin to move from declaration of blessing to status of blessed. We begin to see how God's blessing is worked out in the sin-laden lives of his chosen people. While material wealth is clearly seen and even divinely appointed in the lives of Isaac and Jacob, it is also the source of horizontal conflict with others, such as Abimelech (Gen. 26:14), Esau (27:41), and Laban (31:1–2). What begins to emerge through a close examination of these passages is that blessing and wealth in these narratives cannot be reduced to a simple equation: blessing = wealth.

The book of Genesis presents a world commingled with sin and grace and blessing and curse. Material possessions *can be* the work of God in our lives, or they *can be* the result of sinful envy leading to broken relationships. "Material possessions are not good or evil in themselves, but they must be understood in the context of various relationships; relationships that have been marred, but which can be healed. A world where God remains involved to progress his redemption for all creation."[37] However, the more "earthy" and material nature of blessing in the patriarchal stories also reminds us of the

---

36. Vrolijk, *Jacob's Wealth*, 311.
37. Vrolijk, *Jacob's Wealth*, 299.

creation pattern, and the fact that we are material beings created for life and in need of provision. Divine blessing is not an escape from the material world, and the point of the patriarchal narratives is to show that this earthly provision comes from the one Creator—God. Blessing as material wealth, fertility, and success in the patriarchal narratives must always be understood as an outflow of right relationship with the God who blesses, and this right relationship is mediated through the means of a covenant. The text never presents the pursuit of material wealth as a desirable end in and of itself, and even shows the transformation of Jacob from one stealing a blessing for personal gain to a man clinging to God alone for reconciliation with his brother, blessing, and peace in the land he was promised.[38] Despite the common tendencies of some to read these stories and draw direct parallels to a modern-day pursuit of wealth and prosperity, the stories of the patriarchs drive us back to the covenant promises and the reality of life in God's presence, not just with his gifts.

In the lives of Noah, Abraham, Isaac, and Jacob, we see a tightly organized constellation of blessing that goes on to shape the rest of the Pentateuch. As David J. A. Clines has noted, "The theme of the Pentateuch is the partial fulfillment—which implies also the partial non-fulfillment—of the promise to or blessing of the patriarchs."[39] The themes of land, offspring, and relational presence (that is, blessing) are woven through the rest of the Pentateuch as Abraham's descendants leave Egypt, receive the covenant at Sinai, and head off to the Promised Land.

---

38. Martin Leuenberger, *Segen und Segentheologien im alten Israel: Unterschungen zu ihren religions—und theologie—geschichtlichen Konstellationen und Transformationen*, Abhandlungen Zur Theologie Des Alten Und Neuen Testaments 90 (Zürich: TVZ, 2008), 475.

39. David J. A. Clines, *The Theme of the Pentateuch*, 2nd ed., Journal for the Study of the Old Testament Supplement Series 10 (Sheffield: Sheffield Academic Press, 1997), 30.

3

Covenant Blessing
for God's People

In Matthew 7 Jesus recognizes that parents love to give good gifts to their children. In fact, he assumes this is common knowledge when teaching his followers about how much more his Father loves to give good gifts to his children! As a parent, I love to give gifts to my kids for several reasons—to make them happy, meet their needs, surprise them . . . but most importantly because they're mine and I love them. To borrow Jesus's words, even we "evil parents" understand that gifts to our children are never the ends in themselves (7:11). They are always a means of care and concern, cultivating a familial love relationship. Simultaneously, every child (and all who remember childhood) resonates with the temptation to lose sight of the relationship over the excitement of the present. I can hear my wife sternly instructing my children, "Read the card before you rip open the paper," trying to drive them back to the relational realties that produced their newest trinket.

As we turn our attention from the biblical-theological trajectory of Genesis, we will see Israel as God's son (Ex. 4:23) and the descendants of Abraham experience the blessings promised through the patriarchs—albeit not completely. They will multiply in number, they will be delivered from enemies, they will possess a land, and they will even have a king over them, but all of this will be overshadowed by Israel's sin and unfaithfulness. Israel must fight the temptation to lose sight of their covenant Lord because of their prosperity and blessing. Moses, foreseeing Israel's struggles in the land, warns the people in Deuteronomy 8:11–14, "Take care lest you forget the LORD your God by not keeping his commandments and his rules and his statutes, which I command you today, lest, when you have eaten and are full and have built good houses and live in them, and when your herds and flocks multiply and your silver and gold is multiplied and all that you have is multiplied, then your heart be lifted up, and you forget the LORD your God." The reality is that the Old Testament is a story of Israel's covenant faithlessness and God's continued work despite Israel's sin. And when we ask why God continues to bless his stubborn children, the words of Deuteronomy 7:8 drive us back to the heart of our heavenly Father: "It is because the LORD loves you and is keeping the oath that he swore to your fathers." In this chapter we will walk through much of the Old Testament, witnessing God's love and blessing within the context of the covenant made through Moses.

Covenant Blessings (Exodus–Deuteronomy)

As many commentators note, but too many Bible readers don't know, the Hebrew text of the book of Exodus begins with the conjunction "and." This is significant in that the story of divine blessing unfolding in Genesis is carried forward rather seamlessly into the rest of the Pentateuch. In fact, we come to a clearer understanding of the

promise of blessing to the patriarchs as we work through these subsequent books, so that, as David Clines writes, "At the focal point of
these books, the exodus event and the Sinai revelation, it becomes
plain what the promise meant by its words, 'I will bless you,' 'I will
make my covenant between me and you,' 'I will be your God.'"[1] When
the curtain rises on Jacob's twelve sons living in Egypt, we are immediately made aware of God's blessing on his chosen people: "But the
people of Israel were fruitful and increased greatly; they multiplied
and grew exceedingly strong, so that the land was filled with them"
(Ex. 1:7). God's people, the chosen "seed" of Abraham, is living out
the blessing-commission of Genesis 1:28 and experiencing the promise given through the patriarchs.

As we saw in Genesis, the promised seed will experience threats,
and in the book of Exodus, the threat is Pharaoh. Still, God will
divinely protect and bless his chosen people through the heroic acts
of two God-fearing midwives who didn't fear the king. So, while
Pharaoh is having babies thrown into the Nile, his daughter is "drawing out" Israel's deliverer from that same river. The stage is set for
the divine showdown that will take place between Yahweh and
Pharaoh. The Exodus narrative is a profound demonstration of the
Lord's commitment to protect Abraham's offspring and make himself
known (Ex. 6:6–8). No gods or kings of Egypt would stop Yahweh
from delivering his people from slavery and calling them into the
covenant life in the land he had promised them.

BLESSED IN GOD'S PRESENCE

Israel comes to experience God's blessing in their redemption from
slavery in Egypt, and the book of Exodus grounds this great redemption in the Lord's remembrance of his covenant with Abraham, Isaac,

---

1. David J. A. Clines, *The Theme of the Pentateuch*, 2nd ed., Journal for the Study of the Old
Testament Supplement Series 10 (Sheffield: Sheffield Academic Press, 1997), 50.

and Jacob (Ex. 2:24; 6:5) and in Yahweh's presence among his people. From the burning bush in Exodus 3 to the cloud of glory filling the tabernacle in chapter 40, the theme of God's presence is woven throughout this remarkable narrative of divine protection and revelation. God reveals himself to Moses as the covenant-making God of the patriarchs and promises to deliver the people out of Egypt, leading them to Canaan (Ex. 3:13–17). However, God's deliverance from Egypt is not out of mere covenant obligation to a place—he is bringing his people to himself![2]

Ex. 4:23: "Let my son go that he may serve me."

Ex. 6:6–7: "I will redeem you with an outstretched arm and with great acts of judgment. I will take you to be my people, and I will be your God, and you shall know that I am the LORD your God."

Ex. 19:4: "You yourselves have seen what I did to the Egyptians, and how I bore you on eagles' wings and brought you to myself."

Ex. 20:24: "In every place where I cause my name to be remembered I will come to you and bless you."

God's presence in Exodus is manifested as he delivers and reveals. Israel does experience God's presence at Sinai, and he reveals to them that if they keep his covenant, they will be his "treasured possession" among the peoples and a "kingdom of priests and a holy nation" (Ex. 19:5–6). Christopher Wright comments on the relationship between these pivotal words in Exodus and the promise given to

---

2. "God's people are delivered, in other words, for the same reason humanity had been created: *to dwell with God in the house of God*," (L. Michael Morales, *Who Shall Ascend the Mountain of the Lord? A Biblical Theology of Leviticus*, New Studies in Biblical Theology 37 [Downers Grove, IL: IVP, 2015], 82.)

the patriarchs, saying, "Although the action is taking place between YHWH and Israel alone at Mt. Sinai, God has not forgotten his wider mission of blessing the rest of the nations of the earth through this particular people whom he has redeemed. . . . *Israel is commissioned to be God's people on behalf of the earth which is God's*."[3] Just as we saw in the election of Abram in Genesis 12:1, God's elective choice of Israel does not derail his intention or desire to bless the peoples of earth. As Israel lived the distinctive Yahweh-life, characterized by the divine presence and his commandments, such as remembering the holy and blessed Sabbath day, they would reflect God's good design for his image bearers and mediate blessing to the nations around them. "The abundant life, then, is found in engagement with the divine, in the Sabbath day encounter with God."[4]

In Exodus 33 Moses recognizes that the blessing of the land promised to the patriarchs was not worth having if the Lord was not with them. God tells Moses, "Go up to a land flowing with milk and honey; but I will not go up among you, lest I consume you on the way, for you are a stiff-necked people" (Ex. 33:3). These words reveal the post-golden-calf tension that was mounting between God and his chosen yet rebellious people. Ever since Adam and Eve left the garden, living in God's sinless presence is impossible for sinful people. However, Moses pleads with the Lord, "If your presence will not go with me, do not bring us up from here. For how shall it be known that I have found favor in your sight, I and your people? Is it not in your going with us, so that we are distinct, I and your people, from every other people on the face of the earth?" (Ex. 33:15–16). Israel's blessing and favor before the Lord and before the nations could only be experienced by walking in his presence. Moses understood what

---

3. Christopher J. H. Wright, *The Mission of God: Unlocking the Bible's Grand Narrative* (Downers Grove, IL: IVP Academic, 2006), 225; italics original.

4. Morales, *Who Shall Ascend?*, 48.

many of us struggle to realize, that the greatest earthly gift imaginable loses its meaning apart from a proper relationship to the Lord, leaving us with what the German Romantic philosophers termed *Weltschmerz*—a world-weariness that recognizes the insufficiency of the material world alone to satisfy the deepest desires of the human heart and mind. Because God is gracious and longs to dwell in the midst of his people, he made a way for sinful Israel to experience the blessing of living in his presence—sacrifice.

BLESSING AND SACRIFICE

Israel's God is holy, and they were to be a holy nation set apart and distinct from the nations around them. But as we just noted, difficulty arises when unholy people enter the presence of God. Remember Nadab and Abihu offering strange fire (Lev. 10:1–7)? Israel's sacrificial system is a matter of life and death . . . literally (see Deut. 30:19)! The book of Leviticus offers us far more than ancient rituals and directions for Israelite butchers. More than any other book in the Old Testament, Leviticus reveals the necessity of sacrifice for Israel to experience life in the presence of Yahweh. Bruce Waltke writes, "The sacrifice represents life. . . . The sacrifice offered symbolizes the owner's life and God's ownership and sovereignty of all."[5] When the worshiper brought the animal forward, he would place his hand heavily upon the head of the animal in a "hand-leaning rite," which would "establish some sort of relationship between the offeror and the animal, so that the animal would *be accepted on* the offeror's *behalf*."[6] The animal would then be sacrificed as a substitutionary death, in the place of the worshiper. The result was to be restored communion with God and peace in a relationship threatened by human sin.

---

5. Bruce K. Waltke and Charles Yu, *An Old Testament Theology: An Exegetical, Canonical, and Thematic Approach* (Grand Rapids, MI: Zondervan, 2007), 466.

6. Jay Sklar, *Leviticus*, Tyndale Old Testament Commentary 3 (Downers Grove, IL: IVP Academic, 2014), 90.

The act of covering the worshipers' sins is bound up in the life and blood of the sacrifice. Leviticus 17:11 explains the important relationship between life and blood within the sacrificial system: "For the life of the flesh is in the blood, and I have given it for you on the altar to make atonement for your souls, for it is the blood that makes atonement by the life." Therefore, the exchange of a life for a life "provided atonement for sin and the means of communion between God and his people and they with one another in his presence."[7] This process reached its climax annually on the Day of Atonement, when atonement was made for sins of the nation. Narratively, the prescription of the Day of Atonement in Leviticus 16 follows the recorded death of Nadab and Abihu (16:1). If Israel is to experience life in God's presence, they must do so on his terms and according to his system of sacrificial worship, a system foreshadowing the final act of sacrifice that would secure fellowship, peace, and atonement for God's people once and for all (Heb. 9:11–15).

ISRAEL'S UNSTOPPABLE BLESSING

Before the people leave Mount Sinai, the Lord commissions Aaron and his sons to bless the people of Israel with what has come to be the most iconic Old Testament blessing:

Speak to Aaron and his sons, saying, Thus you shall bless the people of Israel: you shall say to them,

The LORD bless you and keep you;
the LORD make his face to shine upon you and be
gracious to you;
the LORD lift up his countenance upon you and give
you peace.'

---

7. Sklar, *Leviticus*, 466.

> So shall they put my name upon the people of Israel, and I
> will bless them." (Num. 6:23–27)

In this ancient poetic priestly blessing, we see both a depiction of what it meant for Israel to experience God's blessing and the "guarantee that God would indeed *bless the people of Israel.*"[8]

In commenting on this classic blessing, several points are in order. (1) The passage emphasizes that while the priest is God's chosen mediator, God alone is the source and provider of blessing. "This point is made emphatically clear by the threefold use of the divine Name in the blessing formula itself."[9] (2) The instructions for the blessing include "the people of Israel," but the blessing itself contains the second person singular "you," showing both the corporate and individual function of the blessing. The result is a beautiful picture of God's benevolence and blessing that expresses "both the intimate and personal character of the relationship between the Lord and recipients of blessing."[10] (3) There is a symmetry to the three lines of the blessing, which shows the latter part of the line is quite possibly the consequence of the former. So that God blesses us by keeping us, His face shines upon us in His grace, and God lifting his face to us brings peace in his presence. However, all of these concepts are constituent parts of God's blessing toward his people. The Lord's blessing includes protection, gracious favor, and peace. (4) It is no coincidence that the blessing culminates in the people of God experiencing peace in the light-giving presence of God. The notion of God's *shalom*, or peace, is intimately tied to his blessing. Gordon Wenham writes that peace "means well-being,

---

8. Gordon J. Wenham, *Numbers*, Tyndale Old Testament Commentary 4 (Downers Grove, IL: IVP, 1981), 101.

9. Jacob Milgrom, *Numbers*, JPS Torah Commentary (Philadelphia: Jewish Publication Society, 1990), 50.

10. Patrick D. Miller Jr., "The Blessing of God: An Interpretation of Numbers 6:22–27," *Interpretation* 29, no. 3 (1975): 243–44.

health, prosperity and salvation: in short, the sum total of all God's good gifts."[11] (5) In Numbers 6:27 we are once again reminded of the significance of the covenantal context for understanding God's blessings upon Israel. The Lord states, "So they shall put my name upon the people of Israel, and I will bless them." Israel would not and could not experience God's blessing apart from their identity as his people marked out by his name.

Despite the optimistic tone of the Aaronic blessing in Numbers 6, the subsequent chapters of Numbers reveal a rather difficult journey "in the wilderness"[12] toward the Promised Land. Through a series of grumblings, punishments, and simple lack of faith, the first generation of Israel is prohibited from entering the Promised Land. Their refusal to submit to the rule of their covenant King prevented them from experiencing the fullness of life in the land he promised to them. And were it not for the story of an enigmatic prophet named Balaam, we might be tempted to believe that God had abandoned his plan to bless Israel.

As the newly established nation of Israel travels toward Canaan, they intimidate a certain Moabite king named Balak who wants to see them cursed. In order to carry out this curse, he hires a non-Israelite prophet named Balaam, but Yahweh has other plans. The story of Balaam and Balak is strategically placed in the Pentateuch in order to reiterate God's plan of blessing revealed in the book of Genesis. John Sailhamer writes, "Underlying the narratives which tell the story of Balaam is the author's interest in the promise God had made to Abraham."[13] Balak reports that he hires the prophet because "he whom you bless is blessed, and he whom you curse is cursed" (Num. 22:6). It is as if Balaam becomes the prophetic litmus test for

---

11. Wenham, *Numbers*, 102.
12. This is the Hebrew title for the book of Numbers, *bemidbar*.
13. John H. Sailhamer, *The Pentateuch as Narrative: A Biblical-Theological Commentary* (Grand Rapids, MI: Zondervan, 1992), 405.

Genesis 12:3! Is God going to continue to bless this grumbling and murmuring people?

As the narrative unfolds, Balaam travels with the elders of Moab to proclaim a word from Yahweh over the people of Israel. However, to Balak's surprise, Balaam does not curse the people but blesses them four separate times. The first blessing (Num. 23:7–10) describes how God has not cursed the people, but instead made them numerous. The second blessing intensifies by saying, "He has blessed, and I cannot revoke it. . . . The LORD their God is with them" (23:20–21). God has brought his people out of Egypt, and there is no enemy that can stand in his way. The third oracle compares the tents of Israel to lush images of life and abundance. "How lovely are your tents, O Jacob. . . . / Like palm groves that stretch afar, / like gardens beside a river, / like aloes that the LORD has planted, / like cedar trees beside the waters" (24:5–6). The oracle goes on to describe the king who will reign in Israel, saying, "His king shall be higher than Agag, / and his kingdom shall be exalted" (24:7). In comparing the blessing, favor, and kingship in Israel to a garden and trees planted by waters, this oracle draws on common metaphors to describe Yahweh's blessing upon his people. Frequently in the Scriptures we see trees denoting the place where one experiences life in God's presence, such as the tree of life. Trees can represent those who live righteously and are blessed by God (Ps. 1). They can also represent the one who will reign with righteousness and justice (Isa. 11:1–5).[14] The final oracle of Balaam describes a future Israelite king who "shall exercise dominion" (Num. 24:19). "This latter blessing of Balaam is a direct response to the blessing of Jacob."[15] While Balaam's words themselves

---

14. William R. Osborne, *Trees and Kings: A Comparative Analysis of Tree Imagery in Israel's Prophetic Tradition and the Ancient Near East*, Bulletin for Biblical Research Supplement 18 (University Park: Eisenbrauns, 2018), 111–14.

15. Stephen G. Dempster, *Dominion and Dynasty: A Theology of the Hebrew Bible*, New Studies in Biblical Theology 15 (Downers Grove, IL: IVP, 2003), 116.

confirm the promises given to the patriarchs, the blessings from this prophet-for-hire reveal that Israel's covenant King is not confined to work only through his people.[16] The same God who chose Israel as his "special possession" is the sovereign Lord who is working out his will to bless his people. The book of Numbers introduces the reality that the nations, while having a role to play, will never be the final, determining factor in the history of God's people—in the land or out of it.

BLESSED IN THE LAND?

The final book of the Pentateuch opens with the second genera-tion of Israelites perched on the plains of Moab, preparing to enter the Promised Land. More clearly than any other Old Testament book, Deuteronomy lays out the covenant stipulations for Israel, along with the consequent blessings and curses. As Israel prepares to move into the land that God has promised her, Moses continu-ally reminds the people that their life in the land is intimately con-nected to their life in covenant with Yahweh: "I have set before you life and death, blessing and curse. Therefore choose life, that you and your offspring may live, loving the LORD your God, obeying his voice and holding fast to him, for he is your life and length of days, that you may dwell in the land that the LORD swore to your fathers, to Abraham, to Isaac, and to Jacob, to give them" (Deut. 30:19–20). This relationship between covenant faithfulness, curses and blessings, and land provides the theological foundation for the rest of the Old Testament. "Deuteronomy is the centre of the entire

---

16. Much discussion has encircled the prophet Balaam, presenting him as a Mesopotamian diviner, magician, and prophet-for-hire who seems to know Yahweh. While this story reveals God working through this foreign prophet for mercenary purposes, it does not endorse or vali-date Balaam's character or occupation. Nor does it necessitate that the Old Testament endorses a magical view of blessing, absorbed from the surrounding culture where the gods are manipu-lated by the powers of certain individuals. If this communicates anything, it is that Yahweh is not manipulated by Balaam, but actually vice versa.

Old Testament, in terms of both metanarrative and theology."[17] If one wants to quickly determine Israel's spiritual status in the Old Testament, the first question to be asked is, Where are they in relationship to the Promised Land? Stephen Dempster's summary is helpful: "Canaan is the place of blessing, wilderness the place of curse (Deut. 8:7–16)."[18]

Like Adam and Eve, Israel's ability to experience the blessed life Yahweh intends for them in the land rests upon their response to his covenant commands.[19] According to John Walton, Israel's possession of the land "does give them a place to live, but the point is that it is where they will live in the presence of God. Yahweh is going to dwell in their midst in geographical space made sacred by his presence."[20] So, God was calling Israel to experience blessing in the one land, in submission to the one Lord, in obedience to the one law. "And the LORD commanded us to do all these statutes, to fear the LORD our God, for our good always, that he might preserve us alive, as we are this day" (Deut. 6:24). Truly, as Israel was listening to these words from Moses, they were alive, and they were numerous because "the LORD your God has made you as numerous as the stars of heaven" (Deut. 10:22). Israel was living in the reality of God's blessing and fulfilled promise, but not in its total fulfillment. Here we see the rationale behind David Clines's theme of the Pentateuch as the "partial fulfillment" of the promises given to the patriarchs.[21] Israel exists as a great nation, check. Israel is ready and preparing to move into the land God called them to, check. Israel is blessed and is a blessing to

17. Peter J. Gentry and Stephen J. Wellum, *Kingdom through Covenant: A Biblical-Theological Understanding of the Covenants* (Wheaton, IL: Crossway, 2012), 363.

18. Dempster, *Dominion and Dynasty*, 118.

19. Heath A. Thomas, "Life and Death in Deuteronomy," in *Interpreting Deuteronomy: Issues and Approaches*, ed. D. G. Firth and P. S. Johnston (Downers Grove, IL: IVP Academic, 2012), 180.

20. John H. Walton, *Old Testament Theology for Christians: From Ancient Context to Enduring Belief* (Downers Grove, IL: IVP Academic, 2017), 136.

21. Clines, *Theme of the Pentateuch*, 30.

the nations . . . not yet! Bruce Waltke writes, "The irruption of God's kingdom to this glory as developed in the Bible entails God's people in God's place under God's rule to bless the earth."[22] Deuteronomy calls Israel to love and fear her covenant King, and to walk in obedience to his good commands, living in and living out his blessing.

Nowhere in Deuteronomy are these blessings clearer than in chapter 28, where the people are instructed that if they faithfully keep God's commandments "all these blessings shall come upon you and overtake you" (Deut. 28:2). The remainder of the chapter is filled with depictions of Israel's flourishing in the Promised Land: fertility in their crops and livestock (28:4), abundance of food (28:5), safety in travel (28:6), victory in battle (28:7), foreign peoples seeing Israel's relationship to Yahweh and fearing them (28:10), prosperity in womb and livestock (28:11), and wealth (28:12–13). And the following verses (28:15–68) provide a robust list of what seem like antiblessings, or curses (see 28:15–19). Like the portrayal of blessing depicted in the promises to the patriarchs, the overwhelming picture of fertility, prosperity, and victory in these verses has caused some Christians to stumble. Here, more than in Genesis, the abundance and fullness of blessing seem to provide a positive portrayal of human obedience and divine response. Does Deuteronomy 28 teach that God desires his people to be abundant and prosperous, "the head and not the tail"?

First, the covenant blessings of Deuteronomy 28 cannot be separated from the Mosaic covenant established with the people of Israel at Mount Sinai in Exodus and further developed in the book of Deuteronomy. Most scholars recognize the similarities between Deuteronomy and vassal treaties of the ancient world, which frequently included a list of blessings and curses to be applied to the lesser covenant member depending on his loyalty and obedience to

---

22. Waltke and Yu, *Old Testament Theology*, 150, clearly borrowing from Graeme Goldsworthy.

the stronger covenanting partner.[23] Consequently, the blessings and curses of Deuteronomy 28 cannot simply be removed from their covenantal context and applied to those existing outside the Mosaic covenant. Also, the blessings and the curses go together. While it is quite common to hear people claim the promises of blessing found in Deuteronomy 28, the longer list of subsequent curses is generally ignored.

Second, and building on the covenant setting just mentioned, the blessings of Deuteronomy 28 cannot be severed from Israel's unique position as a nation receiving the Promised Land. The blessings and curses recorded in Deuteronomy are inseparably linked to Israel's fruitfulness in the land or punishment outside of the land. Just as Israel had a historic and unique role to play in God's redemptive plan in conquering the land of Canaan, their fruitfulness and prosperity in the land are also uniquely applied to their role as God's covenant people. The Mosaic covenant was a partial or typological fulfillment of the promises given to Abraham, and it was to be lived out—blessings and curses—by the people of Israel in the Promised Land. Like the garden, once again God's people would have the opportunity to experience God's blessing in his presence. While Israel's appropriation of these blessings was entirely conditional and based upon their covenant love and fidelity to Yahweh, their identity as God's chosen people—a people promised Canaan—was grounded in the unconditional promises of God (Gen. 15:12–16).

Lastly, a sound biblical-theological interpretation of blessing in Deuteronomy cannot overlook the fact that the book points prophetically to a future for God's people beyond the conditional blessing/cursing structure of the Mosaic covenant. In Deuteronomy 30 Moses prophetically announces,

23. Richard S. Hess, *Israelite Religions: An Archaeological and Biblical Survey* (Grand Rapids, MI: Baker, 2007), 55–57.

And when all these things come upon you, the blessing and the curse, which I have set before you, and you call them to mind among all the nations where the LORD your God has driven you, and return to the LORD your God, you and your children, and obey his voice in all that I command you today, with all your heart and with all your soul, then the LORD your God will restore your fortunes and have mercy on you, and he will gather you again from all the peoples where the LORD your God has scattered you." (Deut. 30:1–3)

The text goes on to describe a second exodus where the Lord will regather his people to his land and they will once again experience the blessings of prosperity and growth. However, this regathering and new picture of prosperity and life will be accompanied by a spiritual transformation among God's people: "And the LORD your God will circumcise your heart and the heart of your offspring, so that you will love the LORD your God with all your heart and with all your soul, that you may live" (Deut. 30:6).

So, in essence, the book of Deuteronomy presents a conditional covenant of blessing and curse based upon Israel's covenant loyalty but followed by a prophetic picture of God's unconditional commitment to bless his people after "all these things come upon you, the blessing and curse." Deuteronomy always portrays God's blessings as running parallel to covenant obedience, but the difference presented in Deuteronomy 30 is that God is taking it upon himself to ensure that his people will love him. He is going to apply the covenant sign of circumcision to the heart, *so that* his people will fulfill the love-command of the law (see Deut. 6:4–6; 30:6). "Even if and when Israel rebels against him, Yhwh is sovereign to restore Israel their flagging faith and renew their life."[24] The conditional context of blessing and

24. Thomas, "Life and Death in Deuteronomy," 182.

cursing in Canaan is not the final portrait of how God is going to bring about blessing for his covenant people, because the Mosaic law is not the final way that God will relate to his people.

Blessing and Hope

BLESSING OF THE KING

Moving through the Old Testament narrative of the people of Israel, the story develops as Israel enters the Promised Land. The book of Joshua optimistically reports that "not one word has failed of all the good things that the LORD our God promised concerning you" (Josh. 23:14), and the people of that generation confirm their loyalty at the covenant renewal at Shechem at the end of the book (Josh. 24:1–28). Despite the continual struggles of the people to walk in faithfulness to the Lord (Judg. 2:6–23; 1 Sam. 8:4–22), God shows his faithfulness by raising up *his* king to defeat the enemies of his people and to reign over his land. With the reign of David, the royal seed promise of Genesis starts to become clearer, and the themes of blessing, protection, land, rest, and a great name all demonstrate the continuity between God's covenant with David (2 Samuel 7) and his covenant with the patriarchs. The Lord goes on to promise David two things: (1) a son and heir who would reign on his throne and build a temple for the Lord, and (2) an eternal dynasty with one reigning on his throne forever. Whereas the covenant with Abraham, Isaac, and Jacob alluded to a royal figure arising from their offspring, the covenant with David demonstrates that the patriarchal blessing will forevermore be tied to a ruler from the house of David.[25] David's response affirms God's blessing on his line, saying, "For you, O Lord GOD, have spoken,

---

25. In the ancient world, the king bridged the gap between the people, the land, and the divine. In a phenomenon referred to as "corporate solidarity," the king was to be the faithful worshiper *par excellence*, and his faithfulness ensured divine blessing for the land and people.

and with your blessing shall the house of your servant be blessed forever" (2 Sam. 7:29).

The first promise to David comes to fulfillment in the lifetime and reign of Solomon. Despite early conflicts, Solomon's kingdom is confirmed, and we read, "King Solomon shall be blessed, and the throne of David shall be established before the LORD forever" (1 Kings 2:45). At the climax of Solomon's reign, the Queen of Sheba comes to Solomon and is amazed at his wisdom and prosperity. Through Solomon's wealth, wisdom, and power, the nations are experiencing blessing at the royal seed of Abraham's and David's lines. It seems as though our comprehensive picture of blessing has come to its fullness. The people of God were "as many as the sand by the sea" (1 Kings 4:20), they were prospering as a nation, Solomon had established the great land borders from Genesis 15:18, and most importantly, the presence of the Lord had filled the temple. The only problem is that Solomon—a man like his first father, Adam—was not capable of conquering the sin that plagued humanity. According to 1 Kings 11, Solomon amassed hundreds of wives, built pagan worship sites, and did what was evil in the eyes of the Lord.

Interestingly, with the reign of Solomon, we begin to see a mixed picture of wealth and prosperity. In Deuteronomy 17:16–17, we are told that when the people went into the land, they could appoint a king from among their kinsmen, but he should not acquire for himself excessive wives, horses, or silver and gold. However, 1 Kings 1–11 makes it clear that all these warnings were ignored during Solomon's reign. While the excessive gold and horses seem to foreshadow Solomon's fall, the excessive wives are presented as the direct cause and catalyst leading to his lapsing covenant loyalty. The opulence and wealth of Solomon's reign that seemed to display to the Queen of Sheba his blessed status before the Lord also led to his downfall. Solomon's experience of blessing did not rest upon the horses in his stables, the children in his house, the gold in his throne room, or even the divine wisdom he possessed. Instead of blessings, these aspects of prosperity begin to feel more like liabilities leading him to culturally compromise his faith (cf. Ezek. 28:1–10, 17; 31:1–11).

After Solomon, the people of God continued to follow in the ways of their kings, and the sad truth is that the covenant context of Deuteronomy serves as a theological grading scale for Israel's covenant failures. Like Solomon and many kings after him, the people worshiped at the high places, made sacrifices to other gods, practiced divination, and worshiped the idols of the nations (2 Kings 17). In fact, the record of Israel's history from Joshua to 2 Kings reveals the downward spiral of the nation toward their removal from the land. And according to the book of Kings, this was all a consequence of the people failing to obey the words of Moses in Deuteronomy: "They despised his statutes and his covenant that he made with their fathers and the warnings that he gave them" (2 Kings 17:15). The fall of Judah in the south would soon follow, and like Moses said, the people of God were once again scattered among the nations, cut off from the Promised Land. The reality of exile raised some enormous issues with regard to the covenant blessings promised by God: (1) What of the promise to David and the eternal reign of a Davidic heir? (2) What of the promise to live in the land? (3) And what of the relationship to God and his presence in the temple? Such questions drove the theological vision of Israel's prophets from the days of the divided kingdom to the end of the Old Testament era.

A FUTURE OF BLESSING

The prophets were covenant enforcers that called the people of God back to their covenant king. Like ancient prosecuting attorneys, the prophets would stand on behalf of the Lord, indicting the people for their sin, calling them to return and repent, and revealing God's cosmic plan of judgment and restoration. Because of their sin, God's people would experience the reality of the Deuteronomic curses, but because of his unsurpassable grace, judgment and exile would not be the final scene in God's redemptive narrative.

With poetic brilliance, the prophet Isaiah speaks beyond the reality of exile and judgment with words filled with blessing and promise that reverberate with the language of creation and covenant.

> Listen to me, you who pursue righteousness,
> > you who seek the LORD:
> look to the rock from which you were hewn,
> > and to the quarry from which you were dug.
> Look to Abraham your father
> > and to Sarah who bore you;
> for he was but one when I called him,
> > that I might bless him and multiply him.
> For the LORD comforts Zion;
> > he comforts all her waste places
> and makes her wilderness like Eden,
> > her desert like the garden of the LORD;
> joy and gladness will be found in her,
> > thanksgiving and the voice of song. (Isa. 51:1–3)

Israel's future comfort will be found in the covenant faithfulness of those pursuing God with Abraham-like faith. As John Oswalt writes, "God has promised blessing for curse, fullness for emptiness, and Eden for wilderness. Will those who are seeking God believe that?"[26]

The covenant promises given to Abraham are in view in Isaiah 65:15–16, where we are told Yahweh's servants will be called by new names, and "he who blesses himself in the land / shall bless himself

---

26. John N. Oswalt, *Isaiah 40–66*, New International Commentary on the Old Testament (Grand Rapids, MI: Eerdmans, 1998), 335.

by the God of truth." Alec Motyer helpfully summarizes, "Whoever in the world would enter into the blessing designed for him will enter into that blessing in the God of truth."[27] And in Isaiah 65, this picture of worldwide blessing instead of cursing is given the following explanation: "For behold, I create new heavens / and a new earth, / and the former things shall not be remembered" (65:17). As we will see, the blessings and curses of Deuteronomy will not stand forever as the means by which God relates to this people, and the words of Isaiah in this verse will reemerge in the Revelation of John (Rev. 21–22).

The Edenic picture of restoration so often picked up in the Prophets is nothing less than a total reversal from the Babylonian "land of the cursed" where the people of Israel and Judah would eventually settle. The portrayal of Israel's restoration is couched in the language of the land. Israel's world would be transformed from the desert haunt of jackals to spring-soaked gardens (Isa. 35:5–8), and the wandering sheep of Israel would finally experience abundance and rest "on the mountain heights of Israel" (Ezek. 34:14). The Edenic and creation themes associated with the prophets' depiction of Yahweh's blessing speaks to the cosmic scope of the final restoration of the people of God (Isa. 32:15–20). Yes, the exiled community would return to the land, but the prophets envision a restoration that extends beyond the ancient boundaries of Canaan. Hear the somewhat shocking extent of this global vision in the words of Isaiah: "In that day Israel will be the third with Egypt and Assyria, a blessing in the midst of the earth, whom the Lord of hosts has blessed, saying, 'Blessed be Egypt my people, and Assyria the work of my hands, and Israel my inheritance'" (19:24–25).

Ezekiel 37 captures the multifaceted portrait of restoration that coincides with Israel experiencing the fullness of life in the presence

---

27. J. Alec Motyer, *The Prophecy of Isaiah* (Downers Grove, IL: IVP, 1993), 529.

of Yahweh. The chapter opens with the vision of the valley of dry bones. As the prophet prophesies over the bones, they are transformed from dry dusty bones into a living and breathing army. The vision is not simply a prophetic description of resurrection but also a symbol of the spiritual renewal and restoration that God is going to sovereignly carry out in his people. "And I will put my Spirit within you, and you shall live, and I will place you in your own land. Then you shall know that I am the LORD; I have spoken, and I will do it, declares the LORD" (Ezek. 37:14). Israel's life in the presence of the Lord would require the work of the Spirit of God. However, the latter part of the chapter introduces the reunification of God's people in a second exodus where God will "take the people of Israel from the nations among which they have gone. . . . And one king shall be king over them" (Ezek. 37:21–22). This Moses-like shepherd-king is called by the Lord "my servant David" (Ezek. 37:24; see Jer. 23:5), speaking to the present tension and future realization of a king reigning on the throne of David. The chapter continues to communicate how the people will "dwell in the land that I gave to my servant Jacob" (37:25), and God will "multiply" them there. Finally, the passage emphasizes that all of this will take place within God's presence ("My dwelling place shall be with them," 37:27) and be sealed with the promise of an everlasting covenant (37:26; see Isa. 61:8).

Ezekiel 37 does not explicitly state the word *bless*, but it is evident that this passage portrays all the points that make up the theological constellation of divine blessing in the Old Testament Scriptures.[28] Ezekiel, like his prophetic colleagues, portrays a future hope of life in God's presence for God's people grounded in covenant faithfulness and mediated by a new Davidic king. However, there is a new

---

28. Martin Leuenberger, *Segen und Segentheologien im alten Israel: Unterschungen zu ihren religions—und theologie—geschichtlichen Konstellationen und Transformationen*, Abhandlungen Zur Theologie Des Alten Und Neuen Testaments 90 (Zürich: TVZ, 2008), 2.

covenant reality that must be addressed in evaluating the prophets' position on restoration. Texts like Ezekiel 36:27 and Jeremiah 31:33 reveal that the spiritual transformation occurring within God's people was not an attempt to sidestep the law's demands, but actually an attempt to fulfill them: "And I will put my Spirit within you, and cause you to walk in my statutes and be careful to obey my rules" (Ezek. 36:27). God's standards of righteousness and law obedience are not being tossed aside by this hopeful prophetic vision. Instead, Jeremiah and Ezekiel are prophesying that a day would come when God would satisfy the law's demands upon his people by the power of his Spirit, thereby ushering them into the fullness of blessing he had always intended. Christopher Wright comments aptly on the work of the Spirit in Ezekiel 37, the resurrection, and the church: "That which was focused with tremendous resurrection power on Ezekiel's dead bodies, and then on the dead Messiah, is the same power that is available to the ends of the earth to bring life, salvation and the hope of the bodily resurrection to all who trust in the one who sends it."[29]

Blessing in the Psalms and Wisdom

While Israel's prophets critique, rebuke, and warn the people of God during a time of spiritual decline and exile, the Psalms, Proverbs, and Job portray the spiritual complexities of living as God's people in the land of the living. If we are tempted to adopt a simplistic notion of divine blessing where the righteous always have good things and the wicked always suffer, these books shake us free from this theological naivete. Located at the beginning of the third section of the Hebrew Bible, the Psalter and Wisdom Writings present us with a picture of Israel's covenant life and blessing before Yahweh.

---

29. Christopher J. H. Wright, *The Message of Ezekiel*, Bible Speaks Today (Downers Grove, IL: IVP Academic, 2001), 311.

BLESSING IN THE LAND OF THE LIVING

In the Psalms we are introduced to the liturgical formulas that drove Israel's worship before the Lord, and one of those formulas is "blessed be the Lord" (Pss. 31:21; 41:13; 72:18; 89:52). Here we see the reciprocal response of praise from those living and hoping in God's divine blessing. The notion of "blessing" is a reactive declaration of worship and gratitude directed toward the God who blesses. "Thus, when one speaks of blessing in the Old Testament, one must simultaneously consider the dimension of God's praise. Whenever God blesses, those blessed respond with God's praise. Those blessed are, at the same time, those gifted to praise God."[30] To bless the Lord is not to take up some divine power that is to be directed back to the Lord, empowering and supporting him. Christopher Mitchell is certainly right when he says, "God is not praised in order to *elicit* greater blessing from God; he is praised because he has *already* blessed the people."[31] And the Psalms record generations of praise from God's people, with each of the five books of the Psalter concluding with a culminating doxology of praise to the Lord (Pss. 41:13; 72:18–19; 89:52; 106:48; 146–50).[32]

However, the Psalms also describe certain individuals as "blessed." Blessed is the one whose "delight is in the law of the LORD" (Ps. 1:2), "whose transgression is forgiven" (Ps. 32:1), "who takes refuge in him" (Ps. 34:8), "who makes the LORD his trust" (Ps. 40:4), "who dwell[s] in your house" (Ps. 84:4), "who fears the LORD" (Ps. 128:1), and "whose God is the LORD" (Ps. 144:15). It is not coincidental that the book begins with the metaphorical portrait of a righteous, faithful, and

---

30. Reinhard Feldmeier and Hermann Spieckermann, *God of the Living: A Biblical Theology*, trans. Mark E. Biddle (Waco, TX: Baylor University Press, 2011), 272.

31. Christopher W. Mitchell, *The Meaning of BRK "To Bless" in the Old Testament*, SBL Dissertation Series 95 (Atlanta: Scholars, 1987), 171.

32. Mark D. Futato, *Interpreting the Psalms: An Exegetical Handbook* (Grand Rapids, MI: Kregel, 2007), 62.

flourishing tree planted by life-giving streams of water (Ps. 1:3).[33] To experience the state of being blessed is to be properly oriented toward the God of blessing, fearing him, trusting, taking refuge, and experiencing forgiveness. While there are certainly psalms that present divine blessing as fertility and success (like we saw in Genesis), once again these concepts cannot be divorced from their covenant and relational context. Similar to the blessings of Deuteronomy, Psalm 128:1–2 declares that "blessed is everyone who fears the Lord, / who walks in his ways! / You shall eat the fruit of the labor of your hands; / you shall be blessed, and it shall be well with you." Israel was to experience God's blessing, respond in praise, and live in peace and security in the land that their divine King had given them. And like the prophets, the Psalms testify to the pivotal role of the Davidic King—the Messiah—in seeing God's blessing manifested among his people (Pss. 2:12; 18:50; 132:10–18).[34] God's people will be satisfied and blessed in his presence on Zion, and with his Messiah.

> For the Lord has chosen Zion;
>> he has desired it for his dwelling place:
> "This is my resting place forever;
>> here I will dwell, for I have desired it.
> I will abundantly bless her provisions;
>> I will satisfy her poor with bread.
> Her priests I will clothe with salvation,
>> and her saints will shout for joy.
> There I will make a horn to sprout for David;
>> I have prepared a lamp for my anointed.

---

33. The word for "blessed" in Psalm 1 is not the same Hebrew root as *brk*. The word is *ashre* and provides a broader notion of flourishing or personal well-being. However, as the psalm indicates, this notion of flourishing should not be viewed as "secular" or removed from a proper faith response to the word of God. See William R. Osborne, "The Tree of Life in Proverbs and Psalms," in *The Tree of Life*, ed. Douglas Estes, Themes in Biblical Narrative (Leiden: Brill, 2020), 111.

34. Futato, *Interpreting the Psalms*, 80–90.

His enemies I will clothe with shame,
  but on him his crown will shine." (Ps. 132:13–18)

As modern Christians, we tend to read the psalms with a more individualistic perception of life before the Lord, but we should always recognize that the psalmist is still relating to God in the corporate covenantal context of Mount Sinai. For this reason, blessing in the psalms is found in the law. "Keeping the law *is* a blessing, is blessing itself—bound to God's life and will and fullness of character."[35] Psalm 119 communicates that blessing befits those who walk in the law of the Lord, keep his testimonies, and observe his precepts. So, in one sense, blessing in the Psalms cannot be separated from the Deuteronomic covenant categories of blessing and curse that follow the stipulations of the law. One's actions in response to the revelation of God (i.e., one's character) directly affect the way that one experiences the blessing provided through the law, and the same theme is observed in the book of Proverbs (Prov. 3:33; 10:6; 20:7; 29:18).[36]

The book of Proverbs shapes this character-consequence[37] view of life into a dualistic way of interpreting our actions: wise or foolish and righteous or wicked. Wisdom Literature is firmly rooted in creation and the covenant matrix that we have seen throughout the Old Testament's depiction of experiencing God's blessing. Like wisdom, blessing is an idea that has universal and creational aspects,

---

35. Ephraim Radner, "Blessing: A Scriptural and Theological Reflection," *Pro Ecclesia* 19, no. 1 (2010): 10.

36. Raymond Van Leeuwen rightly warns against finding a thoroughgoing "dogmatism" of character-consequence in the book of Proverbs. He points out that there are texts that seem to acknowledge the perceived tension with "the righteous poor and the wicked rich." (See Raymond Van Leeuwen, "Wealth and Poverty: System and Contradiction in Proverbs," *Hebrew Studies* 33 (1992): 25–36. R. N. Gordon has argued that the driving motive of Proverbs is not a self-guided pursuit of health and success, but "a search for a wholeness in life in which these goals are necessary" ("Motivation in Proverbs," *Biblical Theology* 25 [1975]: 49–56).

37. "Wisdom does not simply try to get people to act wisely but rather encourages behaviors that will transform character that leads to good results" (Tremper Longman III, *The Fear of the Lord Is Wisdom: A Theological Introduction to Wisdom in Israel* [Grand Rapids, MI: Baker, 2017], 180).

yet can rightly be understood only in proper covenant relationship to the Lord. Proverbs is not a divine handbook to sort out your neighbor's problems or a list of binding cause-and-effect predictions based upon law-keeping logic. Israel's sages wanted to provide guidance into what a wise life looked like, and "the objective of the teachings was to encourage people to make the right choices and choose a lifestyle of wisdom and righteousness."[38] Live righteously and God will bless. Keep the law and you will prosper. But life often tells us a different story. What happens when this character-consequence view of divine blessing breaks down? What about when God's covenant people live faithfully, trusting in his word, and still experience tragedy and sorrow?

WHEN THE BLESSING DOESN'T COME

The writers of the Psalms and Wisdom books were not naive or simplistic in their understanding of divine blessing. They wrestled with the reality of the wicked experiencing what looked like God's "blessing." In Psalm 73, the writer testifies that God is good, but the writer almost stumbled when he considered how the wicked around him prospered. They are healthy, wealthy, and at ease, yet they are also proud despisers of God. How can this be? They are "blessed," but they are not living faithfully. The psalm goes on to describe the pivotal moment for the psalmist: "I went into the sanctuary of God; / then I discerned their end" (73:17). What appeared to be the divine blessing was actually a slippery slope leading them away from God, because "those who are far from you shall perish. . . . / But for me it is good to be near God" (73:27–28). True blessings, no matter the form, always lead us nearer to God, deepening our relationship with the divine giver. In Psalm 37, the psalmist rec-

---

38. Lennart Boström, "Retribution and Wisdom Literature," in *Interpreting Old Testament Wisdom Literature*, ed. D. G. Firth and L. Wilson (Downers Grove, IL: IVP Academic, 2017), 145.

ognizes that "Better is the little that the righteous has / than the abundance of many wicked" (37:16), and in Psalm 17 the psalmist seeks deliverance from "men of the world whose portion is in this life" (17:14), but finds comfort in knowing "I shall behold your face in righteousness; / when I awake, I shall be satisfied with your likeness" (17:15). Certainly, the psalmist recognizes a distinction here between those who experience wealth and power in this life and those who find satisfaction in God's presence. Willem VanGemeren comments, "The godly do not comfort themselves with the thought of transitory 'blessings.' They will be 'satisfied' with the likeness of God!"[39]

If the Psalms help us discern prosperity, wealth, and fertility accompanying the life of the wicked, the book of Job wrestles with the reality of the righteous suffering instead of experiencing blessing. The book presents Job as a primary candidate for divine blessing, and indeed, the opening chapter confirms God's favor upon Job's life (Job 1:8–10). But the accuser comes and challenges Job's piety and the Lord's worthiness of worship. "Does Job fear God for no reason?" he questions (1:9). He argues that God has bought Job's faithfulness with his blessings. However, should the Lord remove his favor, the accusation is leveled, "he will curse you to your face" (Job 1:11). Interestingly, in these opening chapters, the verb *brk* that we have seen usually communicating blessing is used to denote the idea of cursing (1:5; 11; 2:5, 9). It is as though the book is setting us up to evaluate the meaning of blessing and cursing as the Job story stretches its protagonist's, as well as its readers', understanding of what these ideas mean. Ironically, the accuser's words in 1:11 are verified when the pious and heartbroken Job tears his garments and declares, "Naked I came from my mother's womb, and naked shall I

---

39. Willem A. VanGemeren, "Psalms," in *Expositor's Bible Commentary*, Rev. ed., eds. Tremper Longman III and David E. Garland (Grand Rapids, MI: Zondervan, 2008), 5:200.

return. The LORD gave, and the LORD has taken away; blessed be the name of the LORD" (Job 1:21).

Job remains faithful amid his tragedy, bad advice, and friendly fire. However, everyone in the story is struggling to make sense of Job's experience in light of a Deuteronomic/Proverbial character-consequence view of the world. Job is a good and faithful person who is experiencing tragedy. Why? Job's answer: there must be some injustice on God's part. Job's friends' answer: there must be some hidden sin in Job's life to justify this misfortune. Both answers are operating on a mechanical and faulty view of the character-consequence idea. While the truisms of Proverbs resonate with all created order—God blesses obedience and conformity to his will and judgment befalls the wicked—these ideas cannot be applied in reverse to "exegete" our everyday experiences. As the Psalms show us that prosperity ≠ righteousness, Job reveals that suffering ≠ wickedness.[40] "To suppose that a person suffers because they are a sinner (or that they live well because they are wise, godly, and righteous) is not only wrong-minded but cruel."[41] The book of Job closes with God coming to Job and exposing his misunderstanding with a long list of rhetorical questions. In response, Job admits his lack of understanding and repents in dust and ashes (Job 42:1–6). However, while Job does not emerge from the divine whirlwind with a greater understanding of his circumstances, he does experience a greater degree of God's presence in his life. "I had heard of you by the hearing of the ear, / but now my eyes see you" (Job 42:5). In many ways, this is the theological heart of the book. Craig Bartholomew and Ryan O'Dowd note, "God is indeed good, and his purposes will be accomplished in the end; but this journey must be lived by embracing the mystery and wonder

---

40. It should be noted that even in Proverbs an oversimplistic view of cause-and-effect wisdom needs to be disregarded. In several places the writers emphasize that wisdom with a little is better than success with foolishness.

41. Longman, *The Fear of the Lord*, 182.

of human life in this world."[42] Wisdom is not achieved by applying Proverbs-like logic to the world and parsing all the experiences of success and failure we see around us and in our own lives. It is lived out in humble trust and wonder in the goodness of God's character in times of plenty and want.

The ending of the book of Job presents us with an interesting "happy ending" regarding the topic of divine blessing. We are told that God rebukes Job's friends (Job 42:8) and restores Job's fortunes: "And the LORD blessed the latter days of Job more than his beginning" (42:12). Some have argued that this ending just drives home the faulty understanding of the character-consequence paradigm assumed by Job's friends and undermines the struggle of the righteous sufferer.[43] However, pushing against the tide of prosperity teachings, God's blessing of Job at the end of the story is neither repayment for the trial that Job encountered nor reward for Job's repentance and understanding. It is not meant to teach us that God will always repay us for our troubles in this life. John Hartley is certainly right when he says, "The blessing proves that Yahweh is a life-giving God, not a capricious deity who takes pleasure in the suffering of those who fear him. . . . Moreover, the doubling symbolizes Yahweh's full acceptance of Job."[44] God's restoration of Job was a gracious act of divine blessing demonstrating his approval of Job and a marking that "the text has come to a successful conclusion."[45] Reading and synthesizing the Psalms and wisdom texts of the Old Testament challenges and forces us to examine how we come to evaluate and expect divine blessing in our lives.

---

42. Craig Bartholomew and Ryan O'Dowd, *Old Testament Wisdom Literature: A Theological Introduction* (Downers Grove, IL: IVP Academic, 2011), 155.

43. Carol Newsom, "The Book of Job: Introduction, Commentary, and Reflections," in *New Interpreter's Bible* (Nashville, TN: Abingdon, 1996), 4:636.

44. John E. Hartley, *The Book of Job*, New International Commentary on the Old Testament (Grand Rapids, MI: Eerdmans, 1988), 540.

45. Longman, *The Fear of the Lord*, 61.

Conclusion

In his book *Happiness*, Randy Alcorn offers a helpful warning about over-spiritualizing God's good gifts, which sometimes leads us to a false dichotomy of either loving the giver or the gifts: "What we should say is, 'Seek the giver *through* the gift.' I should appreciate and enjoy a wonderful meal consciously aware that it, and my capacity to enjoy it, are God's gifts to me. . . . His gifts to us are not gods—but they are God's. And God himself is the greatest gift."[46] Consequently, we need not stumble over the Old Testament's depiction of divine blessing as material wealth, health, and success. From the beginning of the Old Testament in Genesis 1, we observed that divine blessing was always intended to be material, spiritual, and relational. These three characteristics shape the theological constellation of blessing throughout the Old Testament, and even the Bible. As creatures of the earth, humanity was created and called to live in a real-world place. Within that place—whether Eden or Canaan—God would meet their material needs for life by providing abundant food, fertile herds, protection, authority, and a heritage. But they were experiencing these blessings as God's covenant people and could only rightly understand those blessings while faithfully and wisely living within the covenant.

Blessing always contained a vertical and horizontal relational aspect, and within those two directions, there was a spiritual and material component of blessing. We must fight the temptation not to take the spiritual and relational components of divine blessing as seriously when reading the Old Testament, because it was Israel's breakdown in this area that led to the removal of the material blessings of the land during the exile. Through the tragedy of exile, Israel came to understand that the material prosperity of the land could

---

46. Randy Alcorn, *Happiness* (Carol Stream, IL: Tyndale House, 2015), 99.

be maintained only through a proper relationship to God. And it was during this time of punishment and curse that God revealed through his prophets that he was still committed to blessing all the families of the earth through Abraham's and David's offspring. The prophets proclaimed that there would be a new covenant in which God's people would come to experience the fullness of life in God's presence, but not because God's people would enter a land—their true King would come to theirs.

4

Every Spiritual Blessing

I remember quite vividly sitting in a small group circle when the question was asked, "If God gives me a car, is he blessing me?" The ensuing volley of answers and lip-biting angst led me to believe that there is a significant lack of clarity about what it means to experience God's blessing in our lives as Christians. Some quickly said, "No, it's not God's blessing because he doesn't bless us *now* like he did in the Old Testament." Others, less committed to this theological shift in the Bible, said they thought it could be his blessing but didn't really know how one could be sure.

I mention this experience not to disparage those involved; in fact, since this meeting, I have had many other interactions with Christians who seem to vacillate between these two responses. The reality is that on the face of it, the Bible seems to present significantly different views of divine blessing and favor from the Old Testament to the New. The former seems focused on the material wealth, health, and success of the faithful, while the latter portrays the most faithful as martyred and imprisoned. The Old

Testament seems to celebrate strength and prosperity, while the New Testament guides believers to give sacrificially and publicly acknowledge weakness. Living on this side of the cross, how do we navigate what appears to be a theological rift in the Bible's portrayal of blessing? The goal of these final two chapters is to present a biblically and theologically informed answer to this pressing question.

Continuing Israel's Story

The first place to begin is with a proper understanding of blessing in the Old Testament. As the previous three chapters have hopefully demonstrated, divine blessing in the Old Testament is not a subtle way of religiously hiding humanity's desire for wealth and prosperity. Anyone believing the Old Testament reveals a crude obsession with material wealth is not reading the Old Testament but listening to the twenty-first-century sirens calling for wealth and ease. The prosperity and well-being associated with the Old Testament portrayal of divine blessing is not presented as an end to be pursued. Unlike what is commonly heard in prosperity circles, you don't go through God to get his blessings. Conversely, we might say you go through his blessings to get to God! God is the end to be pursued because his blessing is experienced only by living in his presence.

So, our starting point for reflecting on the New Testament's portrayal of blessing is the same as where we started in Genesis: God's people living in God's presence, rightly relating to his sovereign reign and experiencing his blessing.[1] Consequently, divine blessing in the Old Testament and New cannot be separated from the kingdom of God. The difference is that the New Testament reveals God's blessing

---

1. Graeme Goldsworthy, *According to Plan: The Unfolding Revelation of God in the Bible* (Downers Grove, IL: IVP, 1991), 99.

through the inauguration of a new covenant for God's people and the hope of a new creation. Thomas R. Schreiner writes, "In the pages of the NT it is made clear that God's promises are fulfilled, the end of the age has come (1 Cor. 10:11), the new creation has dawned, eternal life has arrived, and the new covenant is a reality."[2] Therefore, in order to understand the fullness of life in the presence of God in the new covenant era, we must map the way that Jesus fulfills the Old Testament Scriptures and points toward these new covenant and new creation realities.

Understanding that the New Testament carries forward Israel's story highlights the expectations shaping the first-century Jewish community. The Old Testament does not end on a high note for the people of Israel, and the intertestamental period shaped by Second Temple Judaism reveals a people largely oppressed by foreigners, spiritually corrupt, and culturally compromising. N. T. Wright says, "The fundamental Jewish hope was for liberation from oppression, for the restoration of the Land, and for the proper building of the Temple. This complex of expectations was the direct result of believing on the one hand that Israel's god was the king of the world while facing on the other hand the fact of Israel's present desolation."[3] Israel's identity in an oppressive pagan world was fundamentally shaped by her view of God (monotheism), her view of herself in relationship to that God (election and covenant), and her view of her future in light of the coming kingdom of God (eschatology).[4] Jesus enters into this Jewish world in order to fulfill the old covenant and usher in the end-time blessings of the kingdom.

---

2. Thomas R. Schreiner, *New Testament Theology: Magnifying God in Christ* (Grand Rapids, MI: Baker, 2008), 41.

3. N. T. Wright, *The New Testament and the People of God* (Minneapolis, MN: Fortress, 1992), 299.

4. Wright, *New Testament and the People of God*, 248–68. See also N. T. Wright, *Paul and the Faithfulness of God* (Minneapolis, MN: Fortress, 2013), 609–18.

Jesus as the Fulfillment of Israel's Story

The New Testament begins by demonstrating the genealogical continuity between Jesus, David, and Abraham. Matthew's Gospel starts by confirming to his readers that Jesus is stepping into Abraham's promise of an offspring (Gen. 12:1–3; 15:1–6; 17:6–8) and David's promise of an eternal royal dynasty (2 Sam. 7:16). The incarnate Christ enters the canonical stage, stepping into the covenant framework established in the Old Testament Scriptures. And while the opening verse in Matthew 1:1 throws a spotlight on Jesus as the fulfillment of Israel's covenant promises, the following chapters of Matthew's Gospel confirm this reality. "The essential key to all of Matthew's theology is that in Jesus all of God's purposes have come to fulfillment."[5]

The word *fulfill* in Matthew has received quite a lot of attention from scholars because Matthew uses it to indicate relationships that do not strike us immediately as "fulfillment" in the way we typically use the word. We hear *fulfill* and we might think "met an obligation," "came through on a promise," or even a "realization of prophecy." However, while Matthew's use of *fulfill* has a prophecy/fulfillment element to it, the concept is more in line with a typological or figural fulfillment. Typology "looks for links between persons, events, and things within the historical context of salvation and under the assumption that the same God is at work in the whole story."[6] The Scriptures reveal God's providential reign over his world and the promise-driven progression throughout his covenant dealing with his people. Typology maps the continuity of the divine author throughout the progression of divine revelation, identifying the theological development of these Old Testament types in the New Testament.[7]

---

5. R. T. France, *Matthew*, Tyndale New Testament Commentary 1 (Downers Grove, IL: IVP, 1985), 41.

6. Craig G. Bartholomew, *Introducing Biblical Hermeneutics: A Comprehensive Framework for Hearing God in Scripture* (Grand Rapids, MI: Baker, 2015), 499.

7. Leonhard Goppelt, *Typos: The Typological Interpretation of the Old Testament in the New*, trans. Donald H. Madvig (Grand Rapids, MI: Eerdmans, 1982), 17–18.

Matthew's typological use of the Old Testament and the accompanying fulfillment formula ("this took place to fulfill . . .") drive us toward an understanding that Jesus's birth, life, death, and resurrection stand in continuity with God's plan for his people Israel. However, even when the Old Testament is not explicitly cited, Matthew uses what Richard B. Hays calls a "figural narrative device" to lead "the reader to *read backwards* and to see Jesus as the fulfillment of OT precursors, particularly Moses, David, and Isaiah's Suffering Servant."[8] So, Jesus—God's Son—also comes out of Egypt like Israel (Matt. 2:15); Jesus passes through the waters of baptism (Matt. 3:16) like Israel through the Red Sea; the Spirit of God descends upon Jesus (Matt. 4:1) like the servant in Isaiah 42:1, and it drives him into the wilderness to be tempted for forty days (Matt. 4:2), corresponding to the forty years of Israel's wandering; Jesus then goes up the mountain and authoritatively interprets the law for the people like a new Moses in the Sermon on the Mount (Matt. 5–7). As a second Moses, Jesus declares plainly in Matthew 5:17, "Do not think that I have come to abolish the Law or the Prophets; I have not come to abolish them but to fulfill them." Through both quotation and figural narration, Matthew's Gospel clearly portrays Jesus as the fulfillment of God's old covenant people, "for he ushers in the promises to Israel (restoration and return from exile, the land, etc.), embodies their identity, and completes Israel's role, calling, and vocation."[9] In the same way, the apostle Paul tells the Corinthian church that his message concerning the Christ did not waiver, "for all the promises of God find their Yes in him" (2 Cor. 1:20), a verse we will revisit below.

8. Richard B. Hays, *Reading Backwards: Figural Christology and the Fourfold Gospel Witness* (Waco, TX: Baylor Press, 2014), 38.

9. Brent E. Parker, "The Israel-Christ-Church Relationship," in *Progressive Covenantalism: Charting a Course between Dispensational and Covenant Theologies*, ed. S. J. Wellum and B. E. Parker (Nashville, TN: B&H Academic, 2016), 44.

The Present Blessings of the Kingdom in Christ

Okay, so Jesus fulfilled God's Old Testament promises for Israel. What does that mean for God's people, the presence of God's kingdom, and the reality of God's blessing? When Jesus began his earthly ministry, announcing, "The time is fulfilled, and the kingdom of God is at hand; repent and believe in the gospel" (Mark 1:15), his audience had a kingdom-expectation shaped by contemporary Jewish understandings of Old Testament passages (Zeph. 3:15; Zech. 14:9; Dan. 7:13–14). His listeners "did not ask for a definition of the kingdom. They understood him to be proclaiming the dawn of a glorious new era in which Israel would be exalted and the nations made subservient to Israel's God. . . . The Lord would pour out his Spirit on all flesh, and the promise to Abraham that all the nations would be blessed, to the ends of the earth, would become reality."[10] The coming of Christ was an end-time, eschatological event breaking into the first-century world. The question for those encountering Jesus was not so much "What is he saying?" but "Who is he to say these things?" Or, in the words of John the Baptist, "Are you the one who is to come?" (Matt. 11:3).

John's question for Jesus in Matthew 11:3 makes sense when placed within the kingdom expectations of the Jews encountering Jesus. John is sitting in Herod's prison for the sake of righteously rebuking his sinful lifestyle, likely thinking to himself, *This is not what the kingdom is supposed to look like. I cannot be experiencing the blessings of the kingdom of God.* When the kingdom of God comes, people like John should not be rotting in the dark, dank prison of a pagan ruler! Jesus replies to John's inquiry by telling his disciples, "Go and tell John what you hear and see: the blind receive their sight and the lame walk, lepers are cleansed and the deaf hear, and the dead

---

10. Schreiner, *New Testament Theology*, 45.

are raised up, and the poor have good news preached to them. And blessed is the one who is not offended by me" (Matt. 11:4–6). While many of us would prefer that Jesus say, "Yes, I am the one," his answer is far more biblically-theologically compelling and demands that his listeners decide for themselves, based upon their own observations. He is, in essence, saying, "Don't take my word for it, tell John what your own eyes see . . . the words of Isaiah 35:5–6 and 61:1 are coming to life in front of you!" George Ladd writes, "If God's Kingdom is the gift of life bestowed upon his people when he manifests his rule in eschatological glory, and if God's Kingdom is also God's rule invading history before the eschatological consummation, it follows that we may expect God's rule in the present to bring a preliminary blessing to his people."[11] Jesus draws upon these categories of a messianic kingdom expectation to communicate to John that he is indeed the one ushering in such preliminary blessings of the kingdom.

The words of Isaiah 35:5–6 also point to a prophetic perspective of a new creation that reveals the transformation of a fallen, post–Genesis 3 world. Jesus's miracles were not simply "spiritual healings." He miraculously altered the material world in real time and space. Blind eyes received sight, lame hands were transformed, and the dead were raised. The blessings of the kingdom of God were a reversal of the brokenness of human sin, frailty, and even mortality. Jesus's kingdom ministry was no less than a holistic transformation of reality into a new creation. His ministry met people who were broken both spiritually and physically and brought spiritual transformation and physical healing. Jesus then concludes his comments to John's followers stating the blessed happiness experienced by those who respond rightly in identifying him as the "one who is to come." As the fulfillment of God's promises to Israel, Jesus is the new way

---

11. George Eldon Ladd, *New Testament Theology*, rev. ed. (Grand Rapids, MI: Eerdmans, 1993), 70.

that one encounters the prophesied blessing of life in God's kingdom. Ladd goes on to say, "The Kingdom of God is the dynamic rule of God active in Jesus; it is also a present realm of blessing into which those enter who receive Jesus' word."[12] And as Jesus tells his disciples, "But blessed are your eyes, for they see, and your ears, for they hear" (Matt. 13:16).

In light of the presence of the kingdom of God in Jesus Christ, no longer does one enter into right relationship to God through an ethnic identification with the line of Abraham. Claus Westermann explains that in the New Testament, blessing is always specifically *in Christ*.[13] This fact becomes clear throughout the Gospels as the good news of the kingdom is rejected by the Jews and directed toward the Gentiles—those who respond in faith to Jesus. In Luke 4 Jesus arrives in his hometown of Nazareth on the Sabbath, enters the synagogue, and begins reading Isaiah 61:1–2. He then shockingly states, "Today this Scripture has been fulfilled in your hearing" (Luke 4:21). While no doubt surprised, Luke tells us that everyone "spoke well of him" (4:22) and responded positively to his teachings . . . that is, until verses 28–29, where we are told they were "filled with wrath" and tried to throw him off a cliff! What in the world happened between verses 22 and 28? The people asked him to "bring the same blessings to his own people as he has brought to Capernaum."[14] In response, Jesus reminds them of the ministries of Elijah and Elisha and how they performed miracles for those outside the nation of Israel (1 Kings 17:9 and 2 Kings 5:14, respectively). The implication is that this good news of the kingdom that has been fulfilled in your midst *today* will be experienced by Gentiles, and "just as

---

12. Ladd, *New Testament Theology*, 70.

13. Claus Westermann, *Blessing in the Bible and the Life of the Church*, trans. Keith Crim, Overtures to Biblical Theology (Philadelphia: Fortress, 1978), 65.

14. I. Howard Marshall, *The Gospel of Luke*, The New International Greek Testament Commentary (Grand Rapids, MI: Eerdmans, 1978), 187.

Elijah and Elisha were better received outside of Israel, so the gospel message would receive a better hearing among the Gentiles."[15] Now that Jesus has come as Israel's Messiah, through the line of Abraham and David, the good news of the kingdom is for all of those who receive him.

Jesus's miracles of healing and casting out demons demonstrated to his audience that he was in fact God's Messiah who had come to usher in the kingdom of God. These miraculous deeds, as amazing as they were, served a larger purpose in proclaiming present kingdom realities.[16] Jesus's spiritual encounter in Matthew 12 connects the power of the Spirit to the coming of the kingdom, which was all mediated through a messianic son of David.

The story begins in Matthew 12:22 when a demon-oppressed man is brought to Jesus, and he heals the man. The crowd amazingly wonders, "Can this be the Son of David?" (12:23), because they were anticipating a messiah from David's line who would bring about these blessings of the kingdom. The unbelieving Pharisees, however, indict Jesus for exercising power over demons by being demon possessed himself—a logical quandary Jesus capitalizes upon. After demonstrating the foolishness of their accusation, Jesus replies to his opponents saying, "But if it is by the Spirit of God that I cast out demons, then the kingdom of God has come upon you" (12:28). The power of the kingdom is the power of the Spirit, and the theological "math" of Spirit = kingdom gets worked out through the rest of the New Testament. Where the Spirit of God is at work in the present evil age, the future blessings of the kingdom are breaking in as well. In fact, the presence of the Holy Spirit is the proof presented in Acts 15:8 that the saving grace of God has extended to the Gentiles.

---

15. Robert H. Stein, *Luke*, New American Commentary 24 (Nashville, TN: Broadman, 1992), 159.

16. John P. Meier, *A Marginal Jew: Rethinking the Historical Jesus* (New Haven, CT: Yale University Press, 1994), 2:453.

Where the blessings of the kingdom of God are present, they have been wrought by the power of the Spirit of God.

The Future Blessing of the Kingdom in Christ

A shocking aspect of Jesus's earthly ministry was the inauguration of the kingdom of God on earth, but this is not the only way the kingdom is described in the Gospels. The kingdom of God is also described as a future kingdom that has not yet come in all of its fullness. This tension is frequently referred to by biblical scholars as the already/not yet aspect of the kingdom.[17] While Jesus clearly taught and lived out the present reality of the kingdom of God, he also taught his followers that it was a future inheritance of divine blessing. Describing the second coming of the Son of Man, Jesus says in Matthew 25:34, "Then the King will say to those on his right, 'Come, you who are blessed by my Father, inherit the kingdom prepared for you from the foundation of the world.'" Interestingly, the idea of inheritance here carries us back to the patriarchal covenants and blessings, but the concept has been theologically transformed. To inherit the kingdom is to receive not just the blessing promised to Abraham, Isaac, and Jacob, but the blessing of Jesus's Father. We inherit the kingdom as children through our union with Jesus, or to borrow Paul's language, "and if children, then heirs—heirs of God and fellow heirs with Christ" (Rom. 8:17). Knowing this, it makes sense when Jesus permits the little children to come to him and says, "Truly, I say to you, whoever does not receive the kingdom of God like a child shall not enter it" (Mark 10:15). Like his Father blesses his children, Jesus then lays his hands on the children and blesses them.

After he blesses the children, Jesus is traveling when a wealthy young man asks him what he must do to "inherit eternal life" (Mark

---

17. Meier, *A Marginal Jew*, 451.

10:17; Matt. 19:16). In the exchange that follows, Jesus treats the phrase "eternal life" and "kingdom of God" interchangeably,[18] as he explains to his followers the difficulty of entering the kingdom with wealth: "How difficult it will be for those who have wealth to enter the kingdom of God" (Mark 10:23). The disciples were shocked and asked, "Then who can be saved?" (10:26). This is an interesting question. Why would Jesus's followers be so despairing over a rich person not inheriting the kingdom of God? Most likely, they had accepted a cultural understanding of blessing that grew out of a mechanical view of wealth = blessing and suffering = sin,[19] a position we have already seen addressed by Israel's Wisdom teachers. The rich young man was clearly "blessed," so if he cannot enter the kingdom, who can? The answer: it is only by God's power that one enters God's kingdom. Or, as Eckhard Schnabel says, "Only God can grant eternal life in his presence."[20]

Jesus's instructions to the rich man to "sell all that you have and give to the poor, and you will have treasure in heaven" (Mark 10:21) are not a universal command for all believers to sell all of their possessions (Zacchaeus is proof enough, see Luke 19:8–9).[21] However, we would be foolish not to hear the warning in Jesus's words about material wealth in relation to the kingdom of God. Instead of being proof of God's blessing upon his children, wealth *can be* a stumbling

---

18. The phrase "eternal life" in Mark 10 and Matthew 19 points toward a future-oriented vision of the culmination of the kingdom, whereas in John's Gospel the phrase is often associated with the present reality of the eschatological fullness of life intended for God's people. Colin G. Kruse writes, "The literal meaning of 'eternal life' is the life of the age (to come), but with the coming of the Messiah it is something which may be experienced, in part, in the present age and will be consummated in the resurrection (5:24)" (Colin G. Kruse, *John: An Introduction and Commentary*, Tyndale New Testament Commentary 4 [Grand Rapids MI: IVP Academic, 2017], 34). So, John's use of "eternal life" is quite similar theologically to Matthew, Mark, and Luke's kingdom language.

19. David E. Garland, *Mark*, NIV Application Commentary (Grand Rapids, MI: Zondervan, 1996), 398.

20. Eckhard Schnabel, *Mark: An Introduction and Commentary*, Tyndale New Testament Commentary 2 (Grand Rapids, MI: IVP Academic, 2017), 246.

21. Garland, *Mark*, 402.

block tying us down to the present age. There is an inherent danger in having so much money that all of our felt needs are met in this life. David Garland writes, "The abundance of possessions can easily deceive one into thinking that they offer security and abundant life (see Luke 12:15). Having money beguiles one into believing that everything can be had for a price—even salvation."[22] Jesus calls the rich man to exchange the temporary and fleeting treasures of this world for the eternal and imperishable treasures of heaven (see Matt. 6:19). This is why Jesus speaks so negatively about money in the Gospels (Matt. 6:19–34; Mark 4:19; Luke 12:13–32; 16:1–15). Clinging with undying loyalty to "blessings" (that is, wealth, power, success) in this life can rob people of the eternal blessings they are to inherit in the age to come.

In typical fashion, Peter jumps in and clarifies how much he and the disciples have given up to follow Jesus: "See, we have left everything and followed you" (Mark 10:28). Jesus responds with a significant explanation of self-denial and kingdom blessings:

> Truly, I say to you, there is no one who has left house or brothers or sisters or mother or father or children or lands, for my sake and for the gospel, who will not receive a hundredfold now in this time, houses and brothers and sisters and mothers and children and lands, with persecutions, and in the age to come eternal life. But many who are first will be last, and the last first. (Mark 10:29–31)

Is Jesus teaching us a simple formula that if we give up our possessions, we can receive the kingdom? Is this a divine promise that if you forsake family and lands, God is obligated to restore family and lands, like he did at the end of Job? No. Jesus is apply-

---

22. Garland, *Mark*, 403.

ing a kingdom filter to his disciples' understanding of blessing in the present age. As we saw in the Old Testament, a growing family and fertile land were both ideas frequently associated with divine blessing. However, Jesus redefines these very images based upon a transformed vision of blessing in Christ's kingdom. "Jesus speaks of the extended family of his followers (cf. 3:34–35) with new familial relationship and the sharing of possessions (cf. Acts 2:44–45; 4:32–37)—a new reality whose value is far greater than the security that personal possessions can ever give."[23] Jesus goes on to say that "now in this time" his disciples should anticipate persecutions, but "in the age to come eternal life" (Mark 10:30). The culmination of blessing, the fullness of life in the presence of God, will not be experienced until Jesus's disciples experience eternal life in the age to come, which is portrayed as an anticipated, coming kingdom reality in Mark 10. Despite the dawning of the kingdom in Christ, his followers will still experience persecution and sorrow until that future day, on which "many who are first will be last, and the last first" (10:31).

Happiness in the Reality of an Upside-Down Kingdom

Exploring Matthew's Gospel further, we see the continuation of the relationship between wisdom and fullness of life in Jesus's kingdom teachings. In Matthew 5:2–12 we encounter the beginning of the Sermon on the Mount, often referred to as the Beatitudes (from the Latin *beatus*, meaning "happy" or "fortunate"). While many translations and commentators translate the Greek word in these verses as "blessed are," Jonathan Pennington has demonstrated that this translation fails to conceptually distinguish

---

23. Eckhard Schnabel, *Mark: An Introduction and Commentary*, Tyndale New Testament Commentary 2 (Grand Rapids, MI: IVP Academic, 2017), 245. Paul also seems to appeal to a new, kingdom-oriented view of familial relationships when he refers to Timothy and Titus as his children in the faith (2 Tim. 1:2; 2:1; Titus 1:4).

between the idea of human flourishing and divine favor or blessing.[24] So, when examining the Beatitudes of Matthew 5, we should not read, "God's divine blessing is upon those who mourn, for they shall be comforted." Instead, the emphasis of Jesus's teaching in these verses is on the reality of discipleship in light of Christ's coming kingdom.[25] "Happy" or "fortunate" is the one who lives in light of the kingdom of heaven and allows this future reality to define his or her present experience in the world. Jesus's words are ethical (instructive to his followers) and eschatological (oriented around the coming of his kingdom).

What is striking about the Beatitudes is the discord between the present experience and the kingdom reality. For example, "happy" are those who are poor in spirit (Matt. 5:3), who mourn (5:4), who are meek (5:5), who hunger and thirst for righteousness (5:6), who are persecuted (5:10), and who are reviled (5:11). We naturally think to ourselves, *These are not situations that often lead to perceived happiness or flourishing.* However, not only is the kingdom present in Jesus's ministry, but it is being substantially redefined through his teaching. Commenting on "those who mourn," R. T. France writes, "In God's salvation they will find a happiness which transcends their worldly condition."[26] Jesus's teachings do not provide a simple plan for how to achieve a happy life, and certainly do not list entrance requirements for the kingdom. Instead, similar to Psalm 73, Jesus provides a kingdom-oriented way of understanding the present conditions of living in a fallen world given the present reality of the kingdom of heaven.[27]

---

24. Jonathan T. Pennington, *The Sermon on the Mount and Human Flourishing: A Theological Commentary* (Grand Rapids, MI: Baker, 2017), 41–67.

25. R. T. France, *Matthew*, Tyndale New Testament Commentary 1 (Downers Grove, IL: IVP, 1985), 109.

26. France, *Matthew*, 110.

27. Interestingly, *makarios* is the same word always used in Revelation to describe the "blessedness" of God's people. The Greek word *eulogeoō* is used three times, but only in benedictions directed toward God.

The Beatitudes have a paradoxical ring that sounds similar to other things Jesus says, like "whoever loses his life will save it" (Matt. 16:25). Like the Psalms and Job, Jesus instructs his disciples that things are not always what they seem. There is a way to have "success" in this world that ends in eternal ruin, and there is a way to experience suffering in the present that leads to eternal life. It is not a coincidence that verses 3 and 10 conclude with the declaration of a present truth: "for theirs *is* the kingdom of heaven." The other consequences/results laid out in the passage are future—"for they *shall be* satisfied" (Matt. 5:6)—but "theirs *is* the kingdom." Donald Hagner explains that such language provides assurance of the future, and "this assurance of the future is meant to transform their present existence."[28]

Jesus's teachings on the kingdom are frequently counterintuitive: Die so that you can live. The last will be first. Be happy when you are persecuted. Giving is better than receiving. We do not "intuit" these types of exhortations because in one sense they are alien to the present age in which we live. This upside-down ethics of the kingdom points us to a reality that is not yet fully realized in the present, but ethically shapes us for the kingdom's fullness in the future.

Consequently, there is an already/not yet tension in the experience of God's intended kingdom blessings for his people. As we saw in the Beatitudes, there is a present and very real "happiness" for the people of God that is recognizable to others. Sometimes we are reluctant to use the word *happy* because of its emotionally flimsy feel. However, there remains a profound and blessed happiness for the people of God that transcends circumstance and condition, so that Peter can write, "If you are insulted for the name of Christ, you are blessed, because the Spirit of glory and of God rests upon you"

28. Donald A. Hagner, *Matthew 1–13*, Word Biblical Commentary (Nashville: Thomas Nelson, 2000), 96.

(1 Pet. 4:14). And we come to experience this other-worldly, counterintuitive happiness when the kingdom of God is born into us by the power of God's Spirit (John 3:1–15).

The Spirit and the Blessing

Perhaps no chapter in the New Testament is as important in discussing Jesus's fulfillment of Israel's story as Galatians 3. In twenty-nine verses the apostle Paul weaves together the themes of law, gospel, blessing, and promise to present a coherent vision of how Jesus is the culmination of God's work among his Old Testament people Israel. The chapter opens with Paul's dismay over the struggling Galatian Christians who were being tempted to see Christianity as inseparable from Judaism. "Did you receive the Spirit by works of the law or by hearing with faith?" (3:2), Paul asks his readers. Attempting to demonstrate the centrality of salvation by faith, Paul points the Galatian Christians back to Abraham:

> Know then that it is those of faith who are the sons of Abraham. And the Scripture, foreseeing that God would justify the Gentiles by faith, preached the gospel beforehand to Abraham, saying, "In you shall all the nations be blessed." So then, those who are of faith are blessed along with Abraham, the man of faith. (Gal. 3:7–9)

Like the Gospel writers, Paul clearly interprets Jesus as the fulfillment of God's promise to Abraham in a way that forever redefines the people of God. The blessing promised to Abraham is now realized by all who have exercised faith in Christ Jesus, including Gentiles who possess the Spirit.[29] Paul goes on to say, "So that in Christ Jesus the blessing of Abraham might come to the Gentiles, so that we

---

29. Thomas R. Schreiner, *The Law and Its Fulfillment: A Pauline Theology of Law* (Grand Rapids, MI: Baker Academic, 1993), 129.

might receive the promised Spirit through faith" (Gal. 3:14). The law given through Moses did not have the power to provide life and godliness for the people of God; it was only possible through the power of the Spirit received by faith (3:1–5). Paul describes those Galatian Christians seeking to impose the law as "under a curse" (3:10). This is not because the law was inherently cursed or bad, but because it goes against the new covenant reality that "Christ redeemed us from the curse of the law by becoming a curse for us" (Gal. 3:13).

As a result of what Jesus has accomplished for his people, both the curses and the blessings we encountered in Israel's Scriptures find their fulfillment in Christ.[30] The promised "seed" of Abraham (Gal. 3:16) now mediates God's blessing of salvation and life in the Spirit. And like the sacrifices of old, Jesus's death is a substitutionary sacrifice whereby he takes the curse from us that we deserve (Gal. 3:13). As Christians, we cannot reflect on blessings and curses in the Old Testament Scriptures without coming to understand their fulfillment in Christ.

In the Old Testament, Israel's sacrificial system pointed toward a way for God's people to experience life in his presence, and Israel's land pointed toward a place where God's people could dwell with their Creator. Israel's law also pointed toward an ethical vision of righteousness and wisdom for God's people to live out. Similarly, the Old Testament portrait of blessing pointed toward something greater than merely children, land, health, and money. The material nature of blessing in the old covenant is not inherently wrong, because God has always desired to bless his people materially and spiritually, vertically and horizontally. Just like the law came up short, not because of any inherent problems but because of the spiritual deadness of Israel, God's blessing in the Old Testament continued incomplete because

---

30. Jason DeRouchie, "Is *Every* Promise 'Yes'? Old Testament Promises and the Christian," *Themelios* 42.1 (2017): 30.

of Israel's spiritual failure. The material nature of divine blessing in the Old Testament typologically points toward life experienced in God's kingdom presence, unaffected by the brokenness of sin and death—a life that can be experienced only through faith in the new covenant mediator of blessing, Abraham's seed, Jesus the Messiah.

However, we are still awaiting the final consummation of this type of life, and until then, we find great hope in the present blessings experienced through our life in the Spirit. Paul writes, "Blessed be the God and Father of our Lord Jesus Christ, who has blessed us in Christ with every spiritual blessing in the heavenly places" (Eph. 1:3). Unfortunately, this verse often fuels our antiphysical misconceptions about divine blessing, leading to statements like "God doesn't bless us like *that* anymore." The reason that we have received every "spiritual blessing" in the present is because the reality of the kingdom of God is inseparably tied to the presence of the Holy Spirit in the life of God's people. The "spiritual" nature of new covenant blessings is not connected to a shift from Old Testament material blessings to New Testament spiritual blessings. Instead, it is a shift in redemptive history. Just as we saw in Galatians 3, the problem with the Galatian Christians wanting to live under the law was that they were trying to go back in time. They were living under the "old age." The relationship between the spiritual blessings and the consummation of physical blessings is a matter of redemptive-historical timing.[31]

This does not mean, however, that we no longer experience physical blessings under the new covenant. The point in Ephesians 1:3 is that we have *every* spiritual blessing—that is, in the heavenly places it's all ours! We have yet to experience the same thing in the material world in which we presently live, but it is coming. Jason DeRouchie rightly argues that the problems with the prosperity gospel are two-

---

31. Wright, *Paul and the Faithfulness of God*, 862.

fold: (1) more faith will not always bring wealth and health, and (2) the future promises of God's restored kingdom are not yet present.[32] It is not wrong to read the Old Testament recognizing God's promises to his people, believing they are fulfilled in Christ and his church. The problem is a failure to recognize that the blessings of the kingdom have begun in our new life in the Spirit, but they are not fully here. Thus, faithful Christians suffer from rheumatoid arthritis and mental illness and get diagnosed with cancer. Persecution is real for many brothers and sisters all over the world whose faith profoundly overshadows many in the Western church. Is this God's initial design for his people? No, and neither is it his final plan. But in the already/not yet tension of the kingdom, we are called—like our Savior—to carry our cross first, and in the life to come receive our crown.

The church in the present age is called not only to experience God's blessing through the work of the Spirit, but to be a blessing by the power of the Spirit. Through the ministry of reconciliation afforded us in the gospel, we are called to pronounce the reality of God's kingdom come in Christ, thereby expanding God's covenant blessings promised to Abraham—the reception of "the promised Spirit through faith" (Gal. 3:14). Peter exhorts the church to "bless, for to this you were called" (1 Pet. 3:9), with the result of receiving a blessing. The body of Christ is to mediate the blessings of God to the present age through lives no longer shaped by the passions of the surrounding culture (1 Pet. 2:11–12), but as those who know the reality of God's kingdom blessings, even in the midst of—indeed, fueled by—suffering and trials. Peter writes, "But rejoice insofar as you share Christ's sufferings, that you may also rejoice and be glad when his glory is revealed. If you are insulted for the name of Christ, you

---

32. DeRouchie, "Is *Every* Promise 'Yes'?," 33.

are blessed, because the Spirit of glory and of God rests upon you" (1 Pet. 4:13–14). By the Spirit, we bless and experience blessings, anticipating the day when the glory of Christ will be revealed. Instead of wealth and power revealing Christ's kingdom to the world, Peter explains, when we come to know the blessings of the kingdom in the midst of trial, we thereby bless those around us by allowing our lives to bear witness to the reality of Christ's kingdom.

Let's close by revisiting a fundamental question: "Why did blessing as prosperity and health point toward divine favor in the Old Testament but not in the New Testament?" First, prosperity and health did not *always* point to divine favor in the Old Testament, and even when it did, this could not be separated from the covenant relationship between God and his people Israel. Second, the Old Testament's portrayal of blessing as the fullness of life in the presence of God does not disappear in the New Testament. Just like the prophets foretold, the new covenant would usher in an age of the Spirit so that God's people would experience the fullness of life (that is, a new birth in the Spirit) in God's presence, except the Spirit of Christ would dwell in them! Third, God can still use material wealth, advantage, and health as ways of blessing his people, but as Jesus warns, these things run the risk of throwing off our redemptive-historical time clock. We can live for this world, losing sight of our future inheritance.

So, the question that contemporary Christians should ask when evaluating whether this thing or that circumstance is God's blessing should be: *Does this "blessing" draw me closer to the triune God? Does this need being met bring me nearer to the giver, or is it a distraction?* No perceived "good gift" will ever drive you away from the Lord, because in God's economy that is not good. And Romans 8 tells us that he is working *good* for his people. In God's economy, wealth can be a precursor to judgment (Ps. 73), and poverty can be a sign of godly surrender (Mark 10). However, God can bless the godly with wealth to better meet the needs of others, while sinful decisions can often lead to pain and loss. There is no simple answer to these questions. But God's divine favor—his blessing—always brings us to himself. And the present hope of the believer is that one day God will finish this work and bring all his people to himself once for all.

5

Eternal Blessings

When I was fifteen, my parents purchased a used truck for me to drive, and I can remember sitting in the cab, listening to music in the garage, anticipating the day I would cruise down the road in my own vehicle. Sadly, I can also remember actually hoping and praying that nothing would happen to me before I turned sixteen, because I could not imagine missing out on *real life*—driving my own car! I knew about heaven and believed in the reality of life after death, but my thoughts were more shaped by cultural depictions of people-turned-angels floating on clouds with harps (not very compelling for a fifteen-year-old boy) than the Bible. My truck seemed like a much greater gift to me back then than anything I saw awaiting me as a Christian.

For many of us, the confusion about whether God's blessings are material or spiritual has to do with our failure to understand the future from a biblical perspective—that is, having a biblical eschatology. I frequently assign students to explain God's work of redemption from Genesis to Revelation, and it is always interesting how many descriptions stop at the present time, failing to account for God's work in the future. Our understanding of God's redemptive work too often appears to run its course in individually saving *us* and delivering *us* to heaven when we die. Neither of these ideas is unbiblical or untrue, but neither captures the full scope of God's blessing for the world and his church.

Hope for the Children of God

As we saw in the last chapter, Jesus and the apostles taught that the kingdom of God was inaugurated (i.e., has begun) in Christ's first coming, but we are still awaiting its fullness. *We are waiting for its fullness.* This phrase summarizes how God's children should reflect upon his blessings. We have been given a down payment (Eph. 1:14), or a "firstfruit" of the kingdom harvest in the Holy Spirit, and it is through the Spirit's blessing us that we come to believe we have more coming our way as God's children. This reality is portrayed clearly in Paul's famous discussion in Romans 8.

Writing to the Christian community in Rome, Paul explains in chapter 8 the relationship between the possession of the Spirit and the presence of Christ, the fullness of life given to us by the Spirit, our identity as God's children, and the future inheritance in glory that awaits those who are coheirs with Christ. While the word *blessing* does not occur in this chapter, the portrayal of present and future blessings, by means of the Spirit, is profound. Douglas Moo writes, "The Spirit is best known in his ministry on behalf of Christians. It is those blessings and privileges conferred on believers by the Spirit that are the theme of this chapter. . . . 'The Spirit of life' (v. 2) confers life both in the present—through liberating the believer from both the penalty (justification) and power (sanctification) of sin—and in the future—by raising the 'mortal body' from the dead."[1]

---

1. Douglas J. Moo, *The Epistle to the Romans*, 2nd ed., New International Commentary on the New Testament (Grand Rapids, MI: Eerdmans, 2018), 491–92.

The presence of the Spirit gives life and bears witness that we are heirs in the family of God, and the inheritance guaranteed is nothing less than the promises of God's blessing given to his people in and through Christ.[2] Similar to how Paul speaks in Ephesians 1:3, our present experience of blessing—that is, the fullness of life in God's presence—is mediated through the presence of the Spirit of Christ in our lives. Romans 8:11 demonstrates that the present dwelling of the Spirit is the means for a future resurrection life that will transform our mortal bodies, just as Christ was transformed by the Spirit in his resurrection. However, Paul communicates clearly that the presence of the Spirit—the "firstfruits" of the kingdom—does not mean that suffering and persecution will be absent. In fact, he writes that our status as heirs and children is contingent upon the fact that "we suffer with him in order that we may also be glorified with him" (8:17). Our union with Christ means that his story becomes our story—cross *then* crown. Our perception of divine blessing cannot be removed from the kingdom pattern of Christ. We too will come to live out our lives knowing first the reality of the cross, and then experiencing the shared glory of our inheritance in the age to come.

In Romans 8:18 Paul helps us see that whatever suffering we may be encountering for the sake of Christ does not compare with the future glory that is our inheritance in Christ. What is this inheritance of glory? Paul writes that whatever this future glory looks like, all of heaven and earth are awaiting the revealing of the sons and daughters of God. As God's children, possessors of the Spirit of Christ, the promise of future glory that we will inherit is nothing less than a renewed and transformed cosmic order.[3] In one sense, it is difficult to explain this cosmic transformation in terms that satisfy our modern,

---

2. Moo, *The Epistle to the Romans*, 505.

3. Peter Stuhlmacher, *Paul's Letter to the Romans: A Commentary*, trans. Scott J. Hafemann (Louisville, KY: Westminster John Knox, 1994), 134.

scientific criteria. However, what is plain here is that the theological reality of our redemption (8:23) is inseparably tied into the restoration and liberation of the created world (8:21).

The connection between our future inheritance in glory and the transformation of the created world is quite significant for our understanding of God's blessing. We must recognize that the future blessing we look forward to, the one that overshadows our present suffering, is not an ethereal, otherworldly spirit-existence. It is instead a world that reflects our material, creation-rooted picture of living a new life as God's people. Thomas Schreiner says that Paul "envisions a future salvation that will engulf the entire cosmos and reverse and transcend the consequences of the fall."[4]

Paul continues to reason that the surety of this future should provide a solid hope for the children of God, and that "in this hope we were saved" (Rom. 8:24, see Gal. 5:5). As believers, we should not be embarrassed by the eschatological backbone of our faith. Paul's missionary, pain-filled, theological reflection left him in a position many of us have never experienced. He could not stick his head in the sand of divine blessing, explaining away his imprisonments, beatings, sleepless nights, and thorn in the flesh. Paul suffered; it was real, and he knew it. However, he escaped despair by clinging to a future hope of glory and blessing for the children of God. When pain and sorrow in this present age drive us to long for our future in glory, this is not necessarily a case of giving up on the promises of God, as some may believe. Note how Paul's future orientation transformed his present condition. He did not pray himself out of prison or hope himself into a better-life-now. He did, however, experience joy and thankfulness in chains (Phil. 1:3–8) and was pleased to see how his own imprisonment was building up the

---

4. Thomas R. Schreiner, *Romans*, Baker Exegetical Commentary on the New Testament (Grand Rapids, MI: Baker, 1998), 437.

body of Christ (Phil. 1:12–14). James Dunn notes, "This correlation between the Spirit and hope recurs sufficiently frequently for us to classify hope as one of the primary blessings of the Spirit for Paul."[5] If our notions of divine blessing require freedom from suffering or persecution, then our hope is grounded in the wrong thing, or maybe in the wrong age. Spirit-fueled hope in the future blessings of God transforms our present experience and shapes us for life in the age to come.

God's Good Gifts

Throughout this book we have seen that God's blessings for his people are relational, spiritual, material, present, and eschatological. Neither one of these aspects negates the significance or importance of the others. In Romans 8, as Paul exhorts his fellow heirs with the hope of their future inheritance of glory, he also helps us to see the reality of God's goodness amid our weaknesses. Verses 26–27 assure us that the same life-giving Spirit is going before the Father on our behalf and according to his will. And then verses 8:28–30 present us with a picture of God's unfathomable goodness right alongside his unwavering sovereignty.

It is true that Romans 8:28 has been carried around like a theological scalpel, intended to lop off the doubts and unbelief of those experiencing suffering. However, this unfortunate practice should not blind us to the true beauty of this passage. Instead, we might think of Romans 8:28 like a daily vitamin regimen that strengthens faith and orients our understanding of goodness for the day of trouble. It is in seasons of weakness, when we are wondering if blessing really will come, that we fall back into the good character of our

---

5. James D. G. Dunn, *The Theology of Paul the Apostle* (Grand Rapids, MI: Eerdmans, 1998), 438. He goes on to list the following passages in support of this claim: Rom. 5:2–5; 8:23–25; 15:13; Gal. 5:5; Phil. 1:19–20; Eph. 1:17-18; 4:4.

Father, who is at work. Instead of this verse promising us that only "good things" will happen to us, it reveals that *everything* that happens to us is his good and purposeful calling.

We might respond to this passage by saying, "Well, that's great. How do I know I won't be another Paul sitting in a foreign prison?" The truth is, you don't. When Christ called us to follow him, there were no sorrow-free or antisuffering clauses. In fact, he said our story would reflect his story—cross then crown. Our story is often filled with heartache and sorrow, but then again so was Jesus's. But more importantly, it is a *good* story.

Too often we conclude that the absence of a certain "good gift" in our lives is proof that our Father is not intending good for us, or even worse, that he really is not good. Deep belief in God's sovereignty divorced from his goodness leads to anxiety and fear, not hope. It's almost as though the apostle Paul senses this human reaction and provides the church with one of the most profound and compelling pictures of God's unconquerable love for his children in Romans 8:31–39. He leads into this discussion with a series of rhetorical questions, drawing us into assurance with a rhetorical "call and response":

> "If God is for us, who can be against us?" (8:31). *"No one!"* our hearts cry.

> "He who did not spare his own Son but gave him up for us all, how will he not also with him graciously give us all things?" (8:32). *"He will!"*

> "Who shall bring any charge against God's elect?" *"No one!"* we shout. "It is God who justifies" (8:33).

> "Who is to condemn? . . . Who shall separate us from the love of Christ?" (8:34–35). *"No one!"*

One of these questions stands out amid the others. The theme alluded to in most of these questions is an implied negative—nothing can come against, overcome, bring charge, condemn, or ultimately separate. But the question of 8:32 is different. This verse is a conditional statement that reasons from greater to lesser: If "he who did not spare his own Son, but gave him up for us all" . . . then, "how will he not also with him graciously give us all things?" Leon Morris writes, "The rhetorical question brings out the certainty that God will continue his blessings for the redeemed. He has done the greater thing in giving up his Son; how can he not now do the less?"[6] In essence, if God has already given his Son, why in the world would we think he is going to withhold good things from us? Jesus, not a new house or a healed back, is the proof of God's goodness toward us.

While Romans 8 does not explicitly state the scope of "all things" mentioned in verse 32, there is no reason to limit God's provision in this text to the present.[7] Verses 8:18–25 describe the cosmic scope of the future glory for God's people, and verses 8:37–39 portray the power of Christ's love over life, death, angels, and all creation. In light of these observations, we can rightly understand the "all things" in verse 32 as including "all those blessings—spiritual and material—that we require on the path toward that final salvation."[8] This certainly seems to be Paul's point when writing to the Corinthian church: "So let no one boast in men. For all things are yours, whether Paul or Apollos or Cephas or the world or life or death or the present or the future—all are yours, and you are Christ's, and Christ is God's" (1 Cor. 3:21–23). "All things" includes all things.

---

6. Leon Morris, *The Epistle to the Romans*, Pillar New Testament Commentary (Grand Rapids, MI: Eerdmans, 1988), 336.

7. Richard N. Longenecker, *The Epistle to the Romans*, New International Greek Testament Commentary (Grand Rapids, MI: Eerdmans, 2016), 755.

8. Moo, *Romans*, 541. So also, Colin G. Kruse, *Paul's Letter to the Romans*, Pillar New Testament Commentary (Grand Rapids, MI: Eerdmans, 2012), 360–61.

Some might read this book and think that I have spiritualized the Old Testament promises of God. Others might think that I have not rightly claimed these promises or recognized the blessings God intends for his people today. To these concerns I would offer up Romans 8:32. There is no blessing for the people of God that will not be given. There is no promise that will not be fulfilled. If this verse tells us anything, it is that God is not stingy! He is not withholding good gifts from us—he has already given the most valuable gift ever given!

This is not a diminished view of God's blessings. John Piper describes how Romans 8:32 has supported him throughout his ministry: "I have fought the fight against fear thousands of times in my life by listening to the voice of God say to me personally: 'I did not spare my own Son; therefore, my promise to you cannot fail. I will help you. Go.' And after forty years I bear witness it has never failed. And it never will. The logic of heaven holds."[9] The vision of divine blessing that consists only of health and success in this life is too small for biblical Christianity. He promises to meet us in every need with *good grace-gifts* that will sustain and empower us to live out his kingdom call on our lives. God does not promise you a new car, a better job, or a spouse and kids. He promises you *everything*!

Conclusion

The story that began in Genesis continues to unfold in our own lives and will continue until the consummation described in Revelation 21 and 22. While Paul's eschatological picture in Romans 8 reflects upon the Trinitarian logic of the Father sending the Son and granting us life in the Spirit, John's vision shows us the future of the people of God through the lens of new creation.

---

9. John Piper, "The Solid Logic of Heaven Holds," Desiring God website, March 15, 2012, https://www.desiringgod.org/messages/the-solid-logic-of-heaven-holds.

In this final redemptive vignette, John hears a loud proclamation declaring that God's program of blessing for his people has reached its fulfillment: "Behold, the dwelling place of God is with man. He will dwell with them, and they will be his people, and God himself will be with them as their God. He will wipe away every tear from their eyes, and death shall be no more, neither shall there be mourning, nor crying, nor pain anymore, for the former things have passed away" (Rev. 21:3–4). God will once again dwell with his people, and the covenantal echoes of "they will be his people, and God himself will be with them as their God" remind us that this is the very same plan that unfolded through God's covenants with Abraham and Israel (see Gen. 17:7; Ex. 29:45; Jer. 24:7; Ezek. 11:20; Zech. 8:8). Death is no more, and God's people will finally experience eternal life in his presence.

John describes these individuals in Revelation 22:14 as blessed: "Blessed are those who wash their robes, so that they may have the right to the tree of life and that they may enter the city by the gates." The blessed happiness of the people described is not of their own doing. Greg Beale writes, "It is not the saints' worthiness that makes them fit for the heavenly city. It is rather Christ's worthiness that qualified him to suffer the penalty for their sins, so that they would not be cast outside the city and suffer in the 'lake of fire.'"[10] By the work of Christ, God's people stand vindicated, clothed, and free to take from the tree of life in the heavenly city.

From Genesis to Revelation, God's plan has been to create life for his people in his presence. Our brief study through the Old Testament and into the New has revealed that while the language of divine blessing may change, the biblical focus on the subject

---

10. G. K. Beale, *The Book of Revelation: A Commentary on the Greek Text*, New International Greek Testament Commentary (Grand Rapids, MI: Eerdmans, 1999), 1139.

remains the same. God's plan to bless reached its fulfillment in the son of Abraham, who was the Son of God. For those of us united to Jesus by faith, we are to live as a blessing to the world in this present age while longing for our eternal blessings in the world to come.

Bibliography

Aitken, James K. *The Semantics of Blessing and Cursing in Ancient Hebrew*. Ancient Near Eastern Studies Supplement 23. Louvain: Peeters, 2007.

Alcorn, Randy. *Happiness*. Carol Stream, IL: Tyndale House, 2015.

Alexander, T. Desmond. *From Eden to the New Jerusalem: An Introduction to Biblical Theology*. Grand Rapids, MI: Kregel, 2008.

Alexander, T. Desmond. *From Paradise to the Promised Land: An Introduction to the Pentateuch*. Grand Rapids, MI: Baker, 2002.

Alexander, T. Desmond. "Messianic Ideology in Genesis." In *The Lord's Anointed: Interpretation of Old Testament Messianic Texts*, edited by P. E. Satterthwaite, R. S. Hess, and G. J. Wenham, 19–40. Eugene, OR: Wipf & Stock, 1995.

Anderson, Bradford A. *Brotherhood and Inheritance: A Canonical Reading of the Esau and Edom Traditions*. Library of Hebrew Bible/Old Testament Studies 556. New York: Bloomsbury/T&T Clark, 2013.

Anderson, Jeff S. *The Blessing and the Curse: Trajectories in the Theology of the Old Testament*. Eugene, OR: Cascade, 2014.

Arnold, Bill T. *Genesis*. Cambridge: Cambridge University Press, 2009.

Barr, James. *The Concept of Biblical Theology*. Minneapolis, MN: Augsburg Fortress, 1999.

Barr, James. *The Semantics of Biblical Language*. Oxford: Oxford University Press, 1961. Reprint, Eugene, OR: Wipf & Stock, 2004.

Bartholomew, Craig G. *Introducing Biblical Hermeneutics: A Comprehensive Framework for Hearing God in Scripture.* Grand Rapids, MI: Baker, 2015.

Bartholomew, Craig, and Ryan O'Dowd. *Old Testament Wisdom Literature: A Theological Introduction.* Downers Grove, IL: IVP Academic, 2011.

Beale, G. K. *The Book of Revelation: A Commentary on the Greek Text.* New International Greek Testament Commentary. Grand Rapids, MI: Eerdmans, 1999.

Bennett, Jessica. "They Feel 'Blessed': Blessed Becomes a Popular Hashtag on Social Media." *The New York Times*, May 2, 2014. https://www.nytimes.com/2014/05/04/fashion/blessed-becomes-popular-word-hashtag-social-media.html.

Blenkinsopp, Joseph. *Creation, Un-Creation, Re-Creation: A Discursive Commentary on Genesis 1–11.* New York: T&T Clark International, 2011.

Boesch, Tina. *Given: The Forgotten Meaning and Practice of Blessing.* Colorado Springs: NavPress, 2019.

Boström, Lennart. "Retribution and Wisdom Literature." In *Interpreting Old Testament Wisdom Literature*, edited by D. G. Firth and L. Wilson, 134–54. Downers Grove, IL: IVP Academic, 2017.

Bowler, Kate. *Blessed: A History of the American Prosperity Gospel.* New York: Oxford University Press, 2013.

Carson, D. A. *Exegetical Fallacies.* 2nd ed. Grand Rapids, MI: Baker, 1996.

Champlin, Matt. "A Biblical Theology of Blessing in Genesis." *Themelios* 42, no. 1 (2017): 63–73.

Clines, David J. A. "Theme in Genesis 1–11." *Catholic Biblical Quarterly* 38, no. 4 (1976): 483–507.

Clines, David J. A. *The Theme of the Pentateuch.* 2nd ed. Journal for the Study of the Old Testament Supplement Series 10. Sheffield: Sheffield Academic Press, 1997.

Collins, C. John. *Reading Genesis Well: Navigating History, Poetry, Science, and Truth in Genesis 1–11*. Grand Rapids, MI: Zondervan, 2018.

Crenshaw, James L. *Old Testament Wisdom: An Introduction*. Louisville, KY: Westminster John Knox, 2010.

Dempster, Stephen G. *Dominion and Dynasty: A Theology of the Hebrew Bible*. New Studies in Biblical Theology 15. Downers Grove, IL: IVP, 2003.

DeRouchie, Jason S. "The Blessing-Commission, the Promised Offspring, and the *Toledot* Structure of Genesis." *Journal of the Evangelical Theological Society* 56, no. 2 (2013): 219–47.

DeRouchie, Jason S. "Is *Every* Promise 'Yes'? Old Testament Promises and the Christian." *Themelios* 42, no. 1 (2017): 16–45.

Dumbrell, William J. *Covenant and Creation: A Theology of Old Testament Covenants*. Nashville, TN: Thomas Nelson, 1984.

Dunn, James D. G. *The Theology of Paul the Apostle*. Grand Rapids, MI: Eerdmans, 1998.

Feldmeier, Reinhard, and Hermann Spieckermann. *God of the Living: A Biblical Theology*. Translated by Mark E. Biddle. Waco, TX: Baylor University Press, 2011.

Frame, John M. *Systematic Theology: An Introduction to Christian Belief*. Phillipsburg, NJ: P&R, 2013.

France, R. T. *Matthew*. Tyndale New Testament Commentary 1. Downers Grove, IL: IVP, 1985.

Futato, Mark D. *Interpreting the Psalms: An Exegetical Handbook*. Grand Rapids, MI: Kregel, 2007.

Garland, David E. *Mark*. NIV Application Commentary. Grand Rapids, MI: Zondervan, 1996.

Gentry, Peter J., and Stephen J. Wellum. *Kingdom through Covenant: A Biblical-Theological Understanding of the Covenants*. Wheaton, IL: Crossway, 2012.

Goldsworthy, Graeme. *According to Plan: The Unfolding Revelation of God in the Bible*. Downers Grove, IL: IVP, 1991.

Goldsworthy, Graeme. *Christ-Centered Biblical Theology: Hermeneutical Foundations and Principles.* Downers Grove, IL: IVP Academic, 2012.

Goppelt, Leonhard. *Typos: The Typological Interpretation of the Old Testament in the New.* Translated by Donald H. Madvig. Grand Rapids, MI: Eerdmans, 1982.

Gordon, R. N. "Motivation in Proverbs." *Biblical Theology* 25 (1975): 49–56.

Grüneberg, Keith N. *Abraham, Blessing and the Nations: A Philological and Exegetical Study of Genesis 12:3 in Its Narrative Context.* Beihefte zur Zeitschrift für die alttestamentliche Wissenschaft 332. Berlin: De Gruyter, 2003.

Hagner, Donald A. *Matthew 1–13.* Word Biblical Commentary. Nashville, TN: Thomas Nelson, 2000.

Hamilton, Victor P. *The Book of Genesis, Chapters 1–17.* New International Commentary on the Old Testament. Grand Rapids, MI: Eerdmans, 1990.

Hamilton, Victor P. *The Book of Genesis, Chapters 18–50.* New International Commentary on the Old Testament. Grand Rapids, MI: Eerdmans, 1995.

Hartley, John E. *The Book of Job.* New International Commentary on the Old Testament. Grand Rapids, MI: Eerdmans, 1988.

Hays, Richard B. *Reading Backwards: Figural Christology and the Fourfold Gospel Witness.* Waco, TX: Baylor Press, 2014.

Hess, Richard S. *Israelite Religions: An Archaeological and Biblical Survey.* Grand Rapids, MI: Baker, 2007.

Hinn, Costi. *God, Greed, and the (Prosperity) Gospel: How Truth Overwhelms a Life Built on Lies.* Grand Rapids, MI: Zondervan, 2019.

Horton, Michael. *The Christian Faith: A Systematic Theology for Pilgrims on the Way.* Grand Rapids, MI: Zondervan, 2011.

Horton, Michael. *Christless Christianity: The Alternative Gospel of the American Church.* Grand Rapids, MI: Baker, 2012.

Jenni, Ernst, and Claus Westermann. *Theological Lexicon of the Old Testament.* 3 vols. Translated by Mark E. Biddle. Peabody, MA: Hendrickson, 1997.

Jones, David, and Russell Woodbridge. *Health, Wealth, and Happiness: How the Prosperity Gospel Overshadows the Gospel of Christ.* Grand Rapids, MI: Kregel, 2017.

Kaiser, Walter C., Jr. "The Old Testament Promise of Material Blessings and the Contemporary Believer." *Trinity Journal* 9 (1988): 151–70.

Kaminski, Carol M. *From Noah to Israel: Realization of the Primaeval Blessing after the Flood.* Library of Hebrew Bible/Old Testament Studies 413. New York: T&T Clark International, 2004.

Kidner, Derek. *Genesis.* Tyndale Old Testament Commentary 1. Downers Grove, IL: IVP, 1967.

Klink, Edward W., III, and Darian R. Lockett. *Understanding Biblical Theology: A Comparison of Theory and Practice.* Grand Rapids, MI: Zondervan, 2012.

Köhler, Ludwig. *Old Testament Theology.* Translated by A. S. Todd. London: Lutterworth, 1957. Reprint, Cambridge: James Clarke, 2002.

Kruse, Colin G. *John: An Introduction and Commentary.* Tyndale New Testament Commentary 4. Grand Rapids, MI: IVP Academic, 2017.

Kruse, Colin G. *Paul's Letter to the Romans.* Pillar New Testament Commentary. Grand Rapids, MI: Eerdmans, 2012.

Ladd, George Eldon. *A Theology of the New Testament.* Rev. ed. Grand Rapids, MI: Eerdmans, 1993.

Leuenberger, Martin. *Segen und Segentheologien im alten Israel: Untersuchungen zu ihren religions—und theologie—geschichtlichen Konstellationen und Transformationen.* Abhandlungen Zur Theologie Des Alten Und Neuen Testaments 90. Zürich: TVZ, 2008.

Lincicum, David. "Genesis in Paul." In *Genesis in the New Testament,* edited by Maarten J. J. Menken and Steve Moyise, Library of New Testament Studies 466, 99–116. New York: Bloomsbury T&T Clark, 2012.

Longenecker, Richard N. *The Epistle to the Romans*. New International Greek Testament Commentary. Grand Rapids, MI: Eerdmans, 2016.

Longman, Tremper, III. *The Fear of the Lord Is Wisdom: A Theological Introduction to Wisdom in Israel*. Grand Rapids, MI: Baker, 2017.

Marshall, I. Howard. *The Gospel of Luke*. The New International Greek Testament Commentary. Grand Rapids, MI: Eerdmans, 1978.

Martens, Elmer A. *God's Design: A Focus on Old Testament Theology*. 4th ed. Eugene, OR: Wipf & Stock, 2015.

Martens, Elmer A. "Tackling Old Testament Theology." *Journal of the Evangelical Theological Society* 20 (1977): 123–32.

Mathews, Kenneth A. *Genesis 1–11:26*. New American Commentary 1A. Nashville, TN: Broadman & Holman, 1996.

Mathews, Kenneth A. *Genesis 11:27–50:26*. New American Commentary 1B. Nashville, TN: Broadman & Holman, 2005.

McKeown, James. *Genesis*. The Two Horizons Old Testament Commentary. Grand Rapids, MI: Eerdmans, 2008.

Meier, John P. *A Marginal Jew: Rethinking the Historical Jesus, Volume 2: Mentor, Message, and Miracles*. New Haven, CT: Yale University Press, 1994.

Milgrom, Jacob. *Numbers*. JPS Torah Commentary. Philadelphia: Jewish Publication Society, 1990.

Miller, Patrick D., Jr. "The Blessing of God: An Interpretation of Numbers 6:22–27." *Interpretation* 29, no. 3 (1975): 240–51.

Mitchell, Christopher W. *The Meaning of BRK "To Bless" in the Old Testament*. SBL Dissertation Series 95. Atlanta, GA: Scholars, 1987.

Moo, Douglas J. *The Epistle to the Romans*. 2nd ed. New International Commentary on the New Testament. Grand Rapids, MI: Eerdmans, 2018.

Morales, L. Michael. *Who Shall Ascend the Mountain of the Lord? A Biblical Theology of Leviticus*. New Studies in Biblical Theology 37. Downers Grove, IL: IVP, 2015.

Morris, Leon. *The Epistle to the Romans.* Pillar New Testament Commentary. Grand Rapids, MI: Eerdmans, 1988.

Motyer, J. Alec. *The Prophecy of Isaiah.* Downers Grove, IL: IVP, 1993.

Nemet-Nejat, Karen Rhea. *Daily Life in Ancient Mesopotamia.* Peabody, MA: Hendrickson, 1998.

Newsom, Carol. "The Book of Job: Introduction, Commentary, and Reflections." In *New Interpreter's Bible: The First Book of Maccabees, The Second Book of Maccabees, Introduction to Hebrew Poetry, the Book of Job, the Book of Psalms*, edited by L. E. Keck, 4:319–637. Nashville, TN: Abingdon, 1996.

Osborne, William R. "The Tree of Life in Proverbs and Psalms." In *The Tree of Life*, edited by Douglas Estes. Themes in Biblical Narrative 100–21. Leiden: Brill, 2020.

Osborne, William R. *Trees and Kings: A Comparative Analysis of Tree Imagery in Israel's Prophetic Tradition and the Ancient Near East.* Bulletin for Biblical Research Supplement 18. University Park: Eisenbrauns, 2018.

Osteen, Joel. *Blessed in the Darkness: How All Things Are Working for Your Good.* New York: FaithWords, 2017.

Osteen, Joel. *Think Better, Live Better: A Victorious Life Begins in Your Mind.* New York: FaithWords, 2016.

Oswalt, John N. "בֶּרֶךְ. Knee." In *Theological Wordbook of the Old Testament*, edited by Laird Harris, 1:132–33. Chicago: The Moody Bible Institute, 1980.

Oswalt, John N. *Isaiah 40–66.* New International Commentary on the Old Testament. Grand Rapids, MI: Eerdmans, 1998.

Parker, Brent E. "The Israel-Christ-Church Relationship." In *Progressive Covenantalism: Charting a Course between Dispensational and Covenant Theologies*, edited by S. J. Wellum and B. E. Parker, 39–68. Nashville, TN: B&H Academic, 2016.

Pedersen, Johannes. *Israel, Its Life and Culture.* London: Oxford, 1926.

Pennington, Jonathan T. *The Sermon on the Mount and Human Flour-ishing: A Theological Commentary.* Grand Rapids, MI: Baker, 2017.

Piper, John. "The Solid Logic of Heaven Holds." Sermon given at Beth-lehem College & Seminary, Minneapolis, MN, March 15, 2012. desiringgod.org/messages/the-solid-logic-of-heaven-holds.

Radner, Ephraim. "Blessing: A Scriptural and Theological Reflection." *Pro Ecclesia* 19, no. 1 (2010): 7–27.

Rosner, Brian S. "Biblical Theology." In *New Dictionary of Biblical The-ology*, edited by T. D. Alexander, B. S. Rosner, D. A. Carson, and G. Goldsworthy, 3–11. Downers Grove, IL: IVP Academic, 2000, 10.

Ross, Allen P. *Creation & Blessing: A Guide to the Study and Exposition of Genesis.* Grand Rapids, MI: Baker, 1998.

Routledge, Robin. *Old Testament Theology: A Thematic Approach.* Not-tingham: Apollos, 2013.

Sailhamer, John H. *The Pentateuch as Narrative: A Biblical-Theological Commentary.* Grand Rapids, MI: Zondervan, 1992.

Sarna, Nahum. *Genesis.* JPS Torah Commentary. Philadelphia: Jewish Publication Society, 1989.

Schnabel, Eckhard. *Mark: An Introduction and Commentary.* Tyndale New Testament Commentary 2. Grand Rapids, MI: IVP Academic, 2017.

Schreiner, Thomas R. *The Law and Its Fulfillment: A Pauline Theology of Law.* Grand Rapids, MI: Baker Academic, 1993.

Schreiner, Thomas R. *New Testament Theology: Magnifying God in Christ.* Grand Rapids, MI: Baker, 2008.

Schreiner, Thomas R. *Romans.* Baker Exegetical Commentary on the New Testament. Grand Rapids, MI: Baker, 1998.

Silva, Moisés. *Biblical Words and Their Meaning: An Introduction to Lexi-cal Semantics.* Grand Rapids, MI: Zondervan, 1994.

Silva, Moisés, ed. *New International Dictionary of New Testament Theol-ogy and Exegesis.* 2nd ed. 5 vols. Grand Rapids, MI: Zondervan, 2014.

Sklar, Jay. *Leviticus.* Tyndale Old Testament Commentary 3. Downers Grove, IL: IVP Academic, 2014.

Smith, Christian, and Melinda L. Denton. *Soul Searching: The Religious and Spiritual Lives of America's Teenagers*. New York: Oxford University Press, 2009.

Stein, Robert H. *Luke*. New American Commentary 24. Nashville, TN: Broadman, 1992.

Stuhlmacher, Peter. *Paul's Letter to the Romans: A Commentary*. Translated by Scott J. Hafemann. Louisville, KY: Westminster John Knox, 1994.

Thiselton, Anthony. "The Supposed Power of Words in the Biblical Writings." *Journal of Theological Studies* 25 (1974): 283–99.

Thomas, Heath A. "Life and Death in Deuteronomy." In *Interpreting Deuteronomy: Issues and Approaches*, edited by D. G. Firth and P. S. Johnston, 177–93. Downers Grove, IL: IVP Academic, 2012.

van der Toorn, Karel. "Theology, Priests, and Worship in Canaan and Ancient Israel." In *Civilizations of the Ancient Near East*, edited by Jack Sasson, 3:2043–58. New York: Scribner, 1995.

VanGemeren, Willem A. "Psalms." In *Expositor's Bible Commentary*. Rev. ed. Edited by Tremper Longman III and David E. Garland. Grand Rapids, MI: Zondervan, 2008.

VanGemeren, Willem A., ed. *The New International Dictionary of Old Testament Theology and Exegesis*. 5 vols. Grand Rapids, MI: Zondervan, 1997.

Van Leeuwen, Raymond. "Wealth and Poverty: System and Contradiction in Proverbs." *Hebrew Studies* 33 (1992): 25–36.

Viands, Jamie. *I Will Surely Multiply Your Offspring: An Old Testament Theology of the Blessing of Progeny with Special Attention to the Latter Prophets*. Eugene, OR: Pickwick, 2013.

Vrolijk, Paul D. *Jacob's Wealth: An Examination into the Nature and Role of Material Possessions in the Jacob-Cycle (Gen 25:19–35:29)*. Vetus Testamentum Supplement Series 146. Leiden: Brill, 2011.

Waltke, Bruce K., and Charles Yu. *An Old Testament Theology: An Exegetical, Canonical, and Thematic Approach*. Grand Rapids, MI: Zondervan, 2007.

Walton, John H. *Ancient Near Eastern Thought and the Old Testament: Introducing the Conceptual World of the Hebrew Bible.* 2nd ed. Grand Rapids, MI: Baker, 2018.

Walton, John H. "Eden, Garden of." In *Dictionary of the Old Testament: Pentateuch,* edited by T. D. Alexander and D. W. Baker, 202–07. Downers Grove, IL: IVP, 2003.

Walton, John H. *Genesis.* NIV Application Commentary. Grand Rapids, IL: Zondervan, 2001.

Walton, John H. *Old Testament Theology for Christians: From Ancient Context to Enduring Belief.* Downers Grove, IL: IVP Academic, 2017.

Wenham, Gordon J. *Genesis 1–15.* Word Biblical Commentary 1. Nashville, TN: Thomas Nelson, 1987.

Wenham, Gordon J. *Genesis 16–50.* Word Biblical Commentary 2. Nashville, TN: Thomas Nelson, 2000.

Wenham, Gordon J. *Numbers.* Tyndale Old Testament Commentary 4. Downers Grove, IL: IVP, 1981.

Wenham, Gordon J. "Sanctuary Symbolism in the Garden of Eden Story." In *Proceedings of the Ninth World Congress of Jewish Studies, Division A: The Period of the Bible,* 19–25. Jerusalem: World Union of Jewish Studies, 1986.

Westermann, Claus. *Blessing in the Bible and the Life of the Church.* Translated by Keith Crim. Overtures to Biblical Theology. Philadelphia: Fortress, 1978.

Wilkin, Jen. "Which Promises Are for Me?" *The Gospel Coalition,* January 12, 2015. https://www.thegospelcoalition.org/article/which-promises-are-for-me/.

Williamson, Paul R. *Sealed with an Oath: Covenant in God's Unfolding Purpose.* New Studies in Biblical Theology 23. Downers Grove, IL: IVP, 2007.

Wise, Michael O., Martin G. Abegg Jr., and Edward M. Cook. *The Dead Sea Scrolls: A New Translation.* New York: HarperOne, 1996.

Wright, Christopher J. H. *The Message of Ezekiel.* Bible Speaks Today. Downer Grove, IL: IVP Academic, 2001.

Wright, Christopher J. H. *The Mission of God: Unlocking the Bible's Grand Narrative.* Downers Grove, IL: IVP Academic, 2006.

Wright, Christopher J. H., et al. "A Statement on the Prosperity Gospel." Lausanne Theology Working Group. https://www.lausanne.org /content/a-statement-on-the-prosperity-gospel.

Wright, N. T. *The New Testament and the People of God.* Minneapolis, MN: Fortress, 1992.

Wright, N. T. *Paul and the Faithfulness of God.* Minneapolis, MN: Fortress, 2013.

Zimmerli, Walther. *The Old Testament and the World.* Translated by J. J. Scullion. London: SPCK, 1976.

General Index

Scripture Index

Short Studies in Biblical Theology Series

THE SON OF GOD
AND THE NEW CREATION

GRAEME GOLDSWORTHY

MARRIAGE
AND THE MYSTERY OF THE GOSPEL

RAY ORTLUND

WORK
AND OUR LABOR IN THE LORD

JAMES M. HAMILTON JR.

COVENANT
AND GOD'S PURPOSE FOR THE WORLD

THOMAS R. SCHREINER

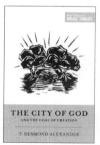

THE CITY OF GOD
AND THE GOAL OF CREATION

T. DESMOND ALEXANDER

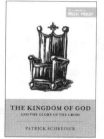

THE KINGDOM OF GOD
AND THE GLORY OF THE CROSS

PATRICK SCHREINER

FROM CHAOS TO COSMOS
CREATION TO NEW CREATION

SIDNEY GREIDANUS

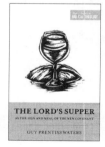

THE LORD'S SUPPER
AS THE SIGN AND MEAL OF THE NEW COVENANT

GUY PRENTISS WATERS

REDEMPTIVE REVERSALS
AND THE IRONIC OVERTURNING OF HUMAN WISDOM

G. K. BEALE

DIVINE BLESSING
AND THE FULLNESS OF LIFE IN THE PRESENCE OF GOD

WILLIAM R. OSBORNE

THE SERPENT
AND THE SERPENT SLAYER

ANDREW DAVID NASELLI

For more information, visit **crossway.org/ssbt**.